Emotional
INTELLIGENCE

Emotional INTELLIGENCE FOR EVERYDAY CHILDREN

TRAUMA

DECISIONS

LOVE

PAIN

HURT

STRESS

IDENTITY

ANGER

EMOTIONS

A SOCIAL-EMOTIONAL GUIDE
FOR EDUCATORS AND PARENTS

XULON PRESS

DR. DENIZELA DORSEY

Xulon Press
2301 Lucien Way #415
Maitland, FL 32751
407.339.4217
www.xulonpress.com

© 2020 by Dr. Denizela Dorsey

Cover Design & Brain Diagrams *MisVision Graphics*
Misvisiongraphics@gmail.com

Library of Congress Control Number: 2020912174
Paperback ISBN-13: 978-1-6312-9788-5
Ebook ISBN-13: 978-1-6312-9789-2

Every day young people grow and learn in communities where trauma, whether mild or extreme, is an everyday way of life. These are our "Everyday Children."

ABOUT THE AUTHOR

Dr. Denizela R. Dorsey is a trained clinical social worker who embraces the "Strengths Perspective." Dr. Dorsey is also an ordained pastor of the Crossing Community Church, who has been providing counseling and psychotherapy services to individuals and families in the Midwest regions of United States (KS, MO, and OK) since 1997. In addition, she is a police chaplain in Saint Louis County. She knows emotional trauma and emotional hardships that interfere with social development, from chronic to complex trauma. Her motto is "**Bringing Restoration and Healing to the Hurting.**" Dr. Dorsey is dedicated to treating those with complex mental illness and trauma, including severe mood, personality, anxiety, and addictive disorders. Dr. Dorsey holds a dual bachelor of science in education and psychology from the University of Southern Mississippi in Hattiesburg. She holds a master of clinical social work from the University of Kansas, a master of divinity from Saint Paul School of Theology in Kansas City, and doctorate of theology from United Theological Seminary in Dayton, Ohio. Dr. Dorsey believes in providing integrated treatment methods to all individuals, regardless of race or gender, while healing the whole person.

Other books written by Denizela R. Dorsey:

One Love One Church: New Voice Cross Racial and Race Relations
Happy Death Day: Lives & Death of UGK's Smoke D: **Memoir**
Two Turntables & A Mixer: Behind the Sounds of UGK with DJ Bird of
UGK: **Memoir**

ACKNOWLEDGMENTS

The *nature of trust* is sacred, and without trust, this work is not achievable. It is done with the confidence of individuals and their families who have allowed me to journey alongside their mental health and emotional pain. From those impacted by Hurricane Katrina in August 2005, to victims of that ravishing E5 Tornado on Sunday, May 22, 2011, at 5:41, in Joplin, Missouri, until this present day, under home quarantines, providing counseling and educational services via Zoom and Skype amidst the COVID-19 pandemic.

These places have watered my gifts: Shawnee Community Mental Health Center, currently known as Valeo Behavioral Health-Topeka, Kansas; Menninger-Clinic, Topeka; and Swope Parkway Comprehensive Health Center, Kansas City, Missouri. Special thanks and gratitude go to Steven L. Unruh, LSCSW, William E. Moore, LSCSW, and Lesia Carter, LSCSW of Topeka, KS, for teaching me how to understand complex mental health conditions while modeling exceptional psychotherapy. This work is complete because of your patience, expertise, and professionalism with my inexperience and questions. Dedication is to all who have ever received a clinical diagnosis, clinical assessment, counseling services, or consultation related to their social and emotional health.

To my precious students and families in Topeka, KS, Kansas City, MO, Webb City-Joplin, MO, Saint Louis County, MO, Cainsville, MO, and St. Joseph, MO: you have made me dig and learn more. Thanks to my professional community of educators, who were a source of inspiration. Those of you who spend countless hours with our students, Kansas City Public School District, Ritenour District-Saint Louis, and AIM High-Saint Louis.

To my son and heartbeat, General, thank you for sharing your mom with so many others. And to my friend and colleague, Zanita Hartzog, one of Georgia's Outstanding Educators, this resource would not be possible without you. Thank you for helping me sort through all of this material and sharping my ideals.

CONTRIBUTORS

David Beck, Cole Chamberlain LLC-DC
Margaret Drummond, Educator-MO
Maria Campbell, Educator-MO
Zanita Hartzog, Educator –GA
Dr. Douglas Petty, Educator, Professional Counselor & Pastor-MO
Clifford McDaniel, Educator-MO
Gwendolyn, Tobias, Educator-MO
Dr. Grayling Tobias, Educator & School District Superintendent
Stacie Wadlington, Educator & Principal-MO
Classroom Pictures, Educator Maggie Drummond-MO

Understanding children and young people are essential and critical! Every day young people grow and learn in communities where trauma, whether mild or extreme, is a daily way of life. Children and Young People are our Legacies for the future and their Mental Health Matters.

Emotional Intelligence for Every Day Children is a Resource Guide for parents and educators packed with relevant result-oriented material that fosters and builds effective relationships while understanding children and young people's psychology.

Emotional Intelligence (EI) prepares you for understanding social and emotional health, strategies to improve instructional practices, and highlights relevant research to address the barriers faced by everyday children that infers with education and emotional development.

ENDORSEMENTS

To you, adults and parents who are working with students,
while navigating through your bubble of trauma.

Educators and Parents,
Remember back to when you were alone and felt challenged, not understanding
what was in front of you. By simply looking back, you can intellectually relate to a
child's view. Before we can assume that our children understand our views, know
how to follow our lead, along with structuring themselves to meet the world in
which they live, let's take a moment to learn, absorb, and understand the psychology of the child's view and how they communicate to us. Whether you are the
subject expert or a parent standing each day alongside your child in the home, the
material written in this **Resource Book** by Dr. Denizela Dorsey makes a difference
and will help you understand clearly how our emotions play a part in reaching a
child and understanding their happiness, pain, and freedom of expression.

As a father and an engineering professional, the emotional intelligence aspect of
digging deeper beyond and understanding the surface misunderstandings that
occur when communicating with my child has made the difference in how we
mutually grow. If you ignore your first gut reactions, you can defeat communication
pitfalls that have a permanent effect positively or negatively on the child's learning,
engaging and interacting with other people for the rest of their lives.

There is a moment in us that we realize that the presence of how we communicate
and with what aspect of the environment we live has a valuable voice in addressing
how we interact and learn in our society...

The works that are presented and meticulously chosen to educate us all are a labor
of love and of will that embodies Dr. Denizela Dorsey every day.

David Beck

Educators,

Imagine driving your car... You can see a bridge ahead... What do you do? A) Drive over the median, sailing into the air? B) Turn the car around and go back? C) Contact your local contractor and have the bridge destroyed? Or, D) Drive effortlessly over the bridge onto the other side? The answer is obvious, right?...

The importance of building relationships is as obvious as the answer to the scenario. The relationship is the bridge. The student is on one side of the bridge, while the educator is on the other. As an educator, I've seen the entire above scenarios take place within the school setting. I've witnessed educators move right past building relationships with students and directly into rules and content. The results are exactly how you'd imagine scenario A's outcome... Warning! You'll want to look away; it's going to get ugly. Too often, some educators resemble scenario B. They try to build relationships, but without much support or guidance on relationship building, they don't know how to focus on the development of that connection and establish meaningful goals that yield tangible results and begin to give up, turn back, and revert to old or traditional ways of educating. Worse yet, there are menaces... I mean, educators who don't believe relationships are important and only aim to "teach" their content; if a student doesn't get the information it is because they are deficient. As in scenario A's outcome... Warning! You'll want to look away; it's going to get ugly.

Relationships are paramount in education; they are the bridges that connect us. To be in a relationship requires an investment, meaning, and purpose. In defining what a relationship is, we must also define what it is not: indifference, detachment, and apathy. To support the structure of a bridge, it must be supported by something. In this case, trust sustains the bridge. With that said, let's go back to the beginning... The importance of building relationships is as obvious as the answer to the scenario. The relationship is the bridge. The student is on one side of the bridge, while the educator is on the other. Scenario D facilitates information that flows both ways, on the bridge, getting ideas and knowledge across to both student and teacher. Without the bridge, knowledge has no passage. Educators, imagine being in your classroom... You can see your students ahead... What do you do? The answer is obvious, right?...

Maria Campbell

TABLE OF CONTENTS

Part One

Part Two

CHARACTER Activity Lessons

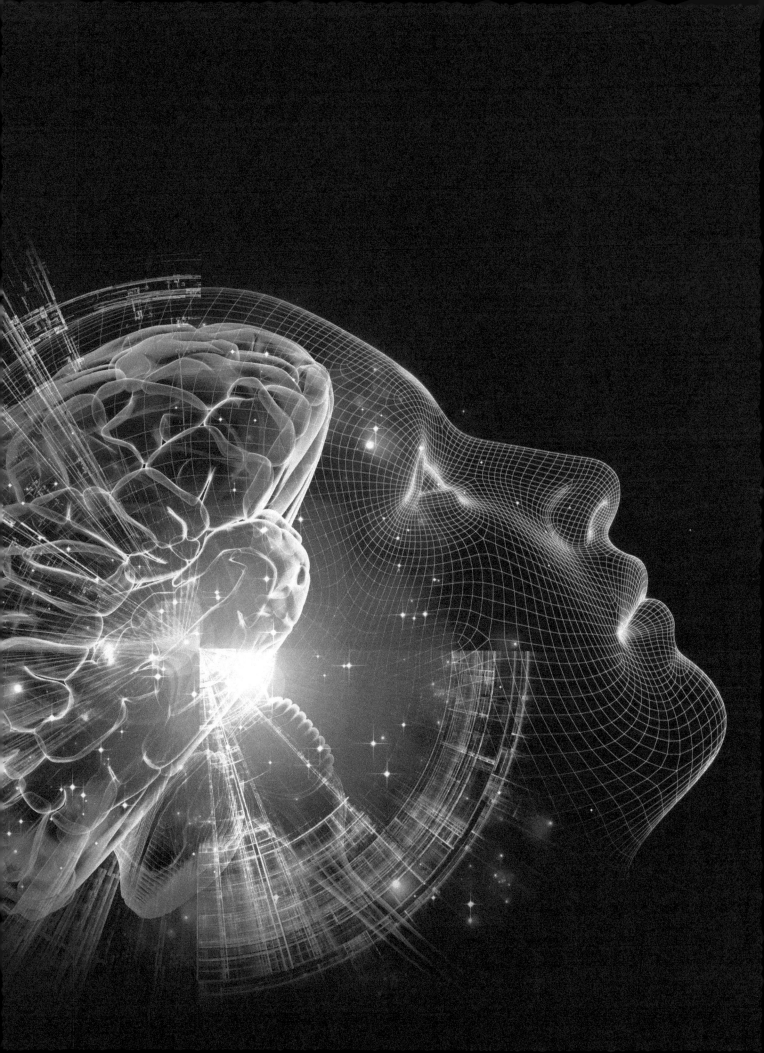

Part One

-As adults we understand that the human reality means experiencing physical and emotional pain, however, children and young people witness it differently.-Dorsey

STORIES PENNED BY EVERYDAY CHILDREN

Anonymous Girl, Age 13

It all started with my mom, dad, and the three of us kids. Everyone was happy which that's what I thought until everything started to show more. My mom was on drugs. She used to cut herself and my dad was a person who sold weed. Going on in life, I started to see the truth about everything, like my sister almost dying at birth due to her lungs almost collapsing because mom beat herself in the stomach when she was pregnant with my sister. There was a lot I still didn't know about everything like my mom going in and out of jail and she wouldn't let my dad come and get us back and forth between two-family homes because my mom couldn't take care of us kids, but at the same time, she never let my dad have us.

Anonymous Boy, Age 13

When I was in preschool I would throw fits. My old teacher has a video. I would get upset and it caused a lot of stress for me. I was only five. And another challenge for my parents was when we lived in a hotel apartment me and my brother were playing tag and I turned around and said "you won't catch me " and then I faced forward and hit my head on the corner of the wall with a large impact splitting it open. My parents were freaking out and to this very day I still have that mark on my head. My stitches did not get taken out until I was six. By the time I was six years old my parents found out I had ADHD. This was another struggle for my parents having to buy me medicine. But when I started taking the medicine, I didn't take the small little tablets. I would fake it. I also had to drink this syrupy stuff. I don't know what it was but it was supposed to help. By the time I hit kindergarten, it was madness with me. I was a mess and I was always in the office until I got to the fifth grade. Once in the fifth grade I got grounded and suspended because I brought a lighter to school. I was burning toilet paper in the school because I thought it was cool. I discovered it was a big mistake. By the time I hit middle school I was super bad. I was always walking out of class having to go see Dr. Dorsey in DWD. All the time it sucked but then my parents thought it was good to go up in a higher dose. I guess the medicine and stupid DWD class was helping. But when I hit seventh grade that bad habit of walking out of class was wearing off because I was tired of going to see Dr. Dorsey. My parents got remarried and that I started carrying around this point sheet that Dr. Dorsey said I needed. I learned in DWD that some kids with ADHD are good at avoiding tasks. Like me, I do it because I can get out of work, to annoy teachers, and when it becomes difficult I just give up. I wish adults would see teenagers are suffering, too.

Anonymous Girl, Age 13

Nope, people hate me and I have come to terms with the fact that I will never be liked, never be loved, nor will my presence make people happy. I'm ok with being alone even though I don't want to be alone, I probably will be. It hurts when you are alone or getting stabbed in the back by your family who is supposed to love you. When people see me and say they hate me at first sight, that's what momma said. I'm happy with that, so don't feel bad for me, I'll make it. Not that it's important anymore. My friends have become everything to me now since my family is so horrible and that is the truth.

Anonymous Boy, Age 11

I thought was raised good, but I learned nothing and took nothing in. My momma and daddy were always fighting my sister and me. I always knew what was coming next when we got yelled at, punishment. They finally split up. The one issue that I had to live with was my dad not being around. When he did come around my mom and dad would always argue and hit each other by throwing things around. I had a lot of anger inside growing up. So when at school when I got mad, I would always scare people by punching stuff, cursing, yelling, and throwing things like my parents. After that, dad stopped coming around. I thought it was because everyone in my family called him a good-for-nothing. Lately, dad hasn't come in a while. He is always in and out of jail. Since 6th grade, I learned about the one thing I need to work on. It's my anger when I get mad, I want to go straight to arguing or fighting. I have been learning how to calm down and ignore people because I don't like to talk my problems out.

All Behavior Is Intentional

A child's behavior can answer many questions, for their behaviors manifest their innermost thoughts, feelings, and overwhelming experiences. Human behavior will always reveal hopes, fears, abilities, and limitations.

INTRODUCTION

Countless hours, in fact, over two decades have been spent with children and young adults with social and emotional traumatizing experiences and those going through a personal crisis. These countless hours include daunting clinical investments of diagnoses, accessing needs, counseling within the therapeutic setting, coaching, and working alongside educators in a trauma-informed school setting. Besides, numerous hours spent teaching parents, advising law enforcement, and educating professionals to help them all understand the simple notion of emotional development, which I call **Emotional Intelligence**. This resource book improves classroom instructional practices in ways that meet the social and emotional needs of the everyday child, highlighting relevant research to support the psychological factors and barriers that everyday children face.

Confronting and growing up in modern-day culture is hugely challenging, socially and emotionally, for nearly all young people today, regardless of their ethnic identity and environment. Their lives are filled with multiple environmental stressors and pressures. Mental depression, anxiety, emotions, and insecurities are what most students confront daily. They struggle to manage and understand the difference between tolerable stress and toxic stress. There is a tremendous pressure of acceptance for young people through social media. They center their lives on the number of **likes** they accumulate. Their need to belong to a specific class or peer group, juggling the demands of home, parents, sports, while performing on a high level of excellence, creates a physical demand on their minds and bodies. Our black and brown children struggle with the emotional hardship related to the systematic effects of racism and discrimination every day. Young people are merely trying to exist in an ever-changing world, which changes instantly with digital technology. Young people are forced to face visual cultural conceptions of violence, war, chaos, and a world that is in constant conflict with self and others.

As teenagers, we adults also struggled at some level with the same notions; some less, some more than others. However, we did not have to navigate the culture of technology. Every child remains the same, but their social and emotional needs differ.[1] The innocence of the young mind is being taken, leading to **teen violence,** which is harmful behaviors that can start early in development and continue into adulthood. The young person can be a victim, an offender, or a witness to the violence. Some violent acts can cause more emotional scars than physical harm.

Violence does not have to be *physical; it* can be *emotional*. Severe *emotional violence* or *emotional disturbance* can alter the way one feels, acts, and responds to the situation. These two causes can lead to severe injury or even death of a young life.

The age of *adolescents* and the term young people have changed, due to new scientific research and studies of the young brain, according to the World's Health Organization. An *adolescent* is defined as the child between the ages of ten and nineteen, while the average age of a *young person* is ten to twenty-four, with the *youth* age being fifteen to twenty-four.

While attending a school function for my son, I heard Frances E. Jensen, MD, University of Pennsylvania Perelman School of Medicine, neuroscientist, say in a 2016 seminar "that the average teenage brain is still going through development until age 25," which means the reasoning skills have not reached capacity.[2] The mind of the average young person is not fully developed, which leads to the moral reasoning and sphere of the young mind being like a sponge, absorbing information from their surroundings. This is possible because the inhibitory and excitatory neurons are responsible for processing sensory information and cognitive functioning. With neurological changes, many young people experience a period of mental illness or emotional distress during childhood or adolescence.[3]

Children experiencing trauma and/or having emotional pain can result in strong emotional responses. Due to the nature of their trauma, it is as similar to those experiencing military combat-related trauma, producing outcomes as manifestations such as anxiety, butterflies, and heart palpitations-tension.[4] About one-third of adults with Post Traumatic Stress Disorder or with strong emotional responses experienced symptoms in childhood, which were often overlooked. Over 25 percent of the PTSD cases are under age fourteen (Hodges et al. 1995).[5] In a recent study conducted before to the COVID-19 pandemic by my assistance superintendent of the Ritenour School District, here in the Ritenour Saint Louis District, found that our middle school through high school students expressed the findings below.

- 23% expressed feelings of overwhelming sadness regularly
- 17.4% felt hopeless about the future
- 28.9% had difficulty concentrating in school
- 17.5% seriously considered suicide in the past twelve months

Sadly, we will probably see a higher number as years progress with all the new transitions and COVID-19 pandemic says Julie Hahn. Knowing this, the emotional intelligence resource book was created.

This resource is infused with insight to create healthy, nurturing, and safe class-rooms. It will improve instructional practices while answering questions to enhance students' social and emotional development. It will build awareness and recognize barriers to learning to offer practical strategies for caregivers, teachers, and coun-selors, which will lead to better-equipped students capable of managing stress and healthy social reasoning. This resource is designed for every student's spheres of moral reasoning to make positive decisions that impact the everyday student in their academic setting. This resource book can be a tool for those who have stu-dents with social-emotional behaviors. This book will help define, understand, and identify a range of emotions while targeting inappropriate behaviors to support academic and personal enrichment in restorative justice practices.

Trauma-Informed comes from the strengths-based framework from the University of Kansas, my ALMA MATER, grounded in an understanding of responsiveness to the impact of **trauma**, that emphasizes physical, psychological, and emotional safety for everyone, and that creates opportunities to rebuild and empower. These practices led me to develop **Emotional Intelligence Learner's Resource**. (*Healthy Brain Power* for short.)

This resource book will address six core areas:

- Biology-Neuroscience
- Psychology-Emotions
- Social Learning and Social Behavior

- CBT-Cognitive Behavior Therapy
- Self-Improvement and Practice
- Mental Illness and Mental Health

Part Two of this resource book will serve as a guide with lessons and activities used in the social and emotional classroom, which refers to Emotional Intelligence Learning Space (**EIL Space**). In the Ritenour School District in my current middle school, after designing the program, administrators named the space *DWD*, which stands for Discipline with Dignity.[6] A year later, after the implementation, Refocus Rooms was initiated.

Part Two will outline the plans for your school to implement an Emotional Intelligence Learning Program or for you to create an EIL Learning Space. The lessons focus on the acronym **CHARACTER**–Easy to remember:

Challenge
Help
Attitude
Respect
Accept
Choose
Trust
Excellence/expectations
Rise

These lessons can be modified to meet your educational setting's needs.

Emotional Intelligence is about changing ourselves and our reactions to the children we teach and serve. It is about changing the lens and filters with which we view and respond to them. Trauma Practices and Restorative Justice are about changing how we treat people and react to the conditions that cause their suffering.

Emotional Intelligence is about Healthy Brain Power. Thanks for reading.

The brain is the last organ in the body to mature.[7] A student's brain is not fully formed until around the age of twenty-five.

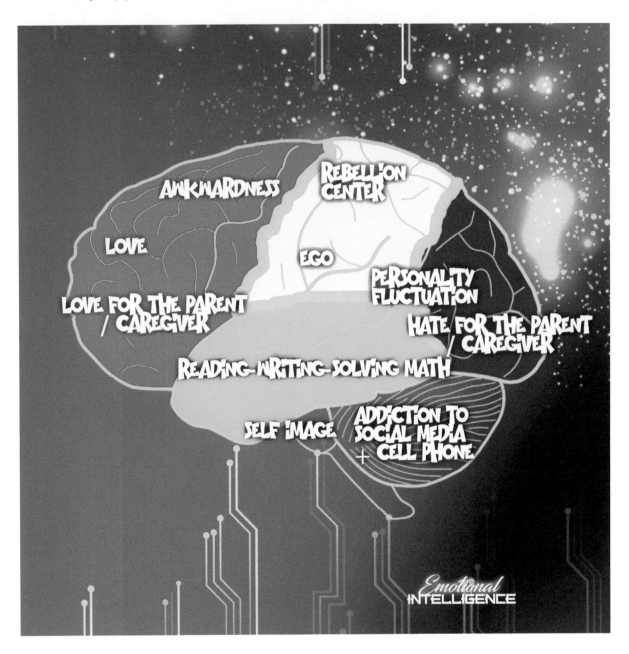

Chapter One

YOUNG BRAIN SCIENCE

Research on the development of the adolescent brain is still ongoing. Just one decade ago, neuroscientists thought the adolescent brain was the same as the adult brain, and by puberty, the growth process was almost complete. This belief led to underfunded scientific research for young brain study. As a therapist who studied psychology and human behavior, the human brain has always fascinated me, how our actions feelings, and thoughts contain the secrets to our true identity.

The ages of ten to nineteen are a time of significant growth and development inside the teenage brain, often referred to as adolescence. The processing power and memory for the adolescent peaks at the age of eighteen, actively keeping the brain in a growth-learning mode. The brain is the last organ in the human body to mature and develop. With understanding that a young brain has uneven regional development, a child's brain may struggle with having the skill sets to be successful with some decision making or self-regulation: controlling his or her emotions while managing his or her thinking. Because of this, a child may tend to explore riskier behaviors than a mature developed brain. A child may be more impulsive or irrational at times. Students become more sensitive to the rewards of peer relationships instead of making the right choices. The scientific reasons for these sensitivities are that the child's frontal lobe (the white matter) or their prefrontal cortex, which is the seat of executive reasoning, is immature and plastic, which influences the young brain to have an increased interest in peer relationship and thrill-seeking behaviors.[8]

Although science has discovered that the bulk of brain development occurs in the womb, the brain continues to develop after birth. In the first five years of a child's development, there is an overall expansion of brain volume related to the development of both gray matter and white matter structures. However, from seven to seventeen years of age, there is a progressive increase in white matter (felt to be related to ongoing myelination) and decrease in gray matter (perceived to be related to neuronal pruning) while overall brain size stays the same (Paus et al. 1999).[9]

The young brain is more active than the adult brain and can be considered as a powerful computer, processing two times more information than their parent or caregiver. When my son was five, he attended Paseo Learning Academy in Kansas City, Missouri. His seventy-five-year-old school master would refer to their brains as little natural computers. Mrs. Erma Williams would graciously remind her students to read each night at least fifteen minutes, get the proper rest, and eat a nutritious meal so that their computer may function adequately. Their persistence with students at Paseo made Paseo Learning Academy a learning warehouse of achievements and emotional intelligence (brainpower).

As the computer works, a young brain is two times more active than the adult brain and can learn at a faster rate than an adult, also referred to as crystallized intelligence. This theory can be tested when a child hears a song one time on the radio and remembers all the lyrics. Adolescents have more synapses than adults. A child's brain produces more synapses than needed; they have more connections per neurons. [10]The human brain creates around 86 billion neurons (nerve cells), with 16 billion neurons in the cerebral cortex. Adolescents are learning machines, and their brains are always creating new memories for connections. During the learning process, the adolescent develops a bigger synapse. The most recent brain research shows that during adolescence, a student's IQ score can change. Below are the measurements of the IQ scores based intelligence and mental competency:

IQ score measurements

- 1 to 24: Profound mental disability.
- 25 to 39: Severe mental disability.
- 40 to 54: Moderate mental disability.
- 55 to 69: Mild mental disability.
- 70 to 84: Borderline mental disability.
- 85 to 114: Average intelligence.
- 115 to 129: Above average or bright.
- 130 to 144: Moderately gifted.

Generally, the IQ score gauges a person's reasoning and problem-solving skills. Ole Rogeberg, an International Research Fellow from Norway, has been studying the IQ's effectiveness and its reversal for a three decade cycle. Rogeberg's study produced astounding results called the Flynn effect. A CNN report aired June 14, 2018, using Rogeberg's data suggests that IQ scores have been steadily declining for the past few decades, and environmental factors are to blame, not genetics. Rogeberg indicates that the environmental factors that impact IQ could include changes in the education system, the social media environment, and nutrition, reading less, and being online more. "Intelligence is heritable, and access to education is currently the most conclusive factor explaining disparities in intelligence."[11]

According to American psychologists, most people (about 68 percent) have an IQ between 85 and 115. This is considered the average of modern-day intelligence. Only small fractions of people have a very low IQ, below 70, or very high IQ, above 130. Hong Kong, Singapore, and South Korea have the most top IQ scores, averaging around 115 for the nation.

Positive factors associated with higher IQ include:

- good nutrition
- regular schooling of good quality education with strong attendance
- laws requiring fortification of certain food products
- laws establishing safe levels of pollutants, like lead
- musical training in childhood
- economic
- lower incidence of infectious diseases

Teenagers' brains are **more** active than that of their adult parents and teachers. Since the frontal lobe is not fully connected or fully formed, **parents, teachers, and guardians** are to be the assisters of the frontal lobe. Every child needs a mature and caring adult to help in making the right decisions. Research shows that academic enrichment activities will support the development of the adolescent brain (Huang, Gribbons, Kim, Lee, & Baker, 2000; Welsh et al., 2002).[12] A student who reads and writes more subsequently influences positive changes in the brain that has a lasting effect on their IQ and development.

For example, a teenager's brain can be compared to a Bugatti Chiron Super Sport with weak brakes. The Bugatti is listed and rated as the fastest car in the world. Teenagers are less likely to modify or stop to change the behavior, and they like the thrill of the ride. They tend to rely on their intuitive nature. Neuroscientist Paul MacLean calls it the Reptilian Complex. Instinct drives this nature of the brain, like most reptiles that do not fear but rely wholly on habit and instinct.

When a child experiences some form of trauma, that trauma disrupts their natural computers, neurological, psychological, and emotional development. **Chapter Two** will discuss trauma with greater detail.

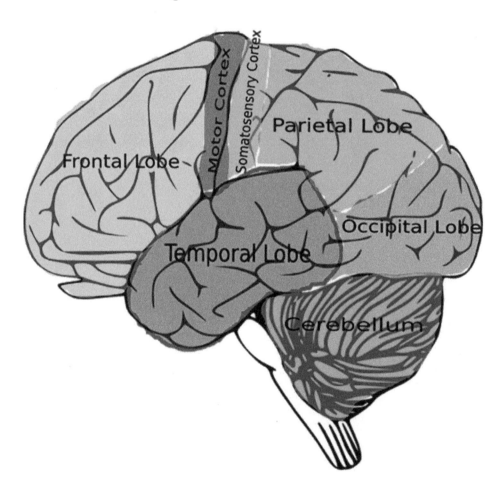

Points to remember and understand about a young brain.

1. Wired to learn
2. Brain very plastic, can change rapidly **"for the better and worse."**
3. Wired to novelty seeking
4. Risk-taking and risky behavior are an inevitable part of the process
5. Connectivity between brain areas not completely formed for complex, split-second decision making; not strong enough in some decisions
6. High emotional liability

Strategies for Educators and Parents

✓ When dealing with a teenager, quote and speak facts. Teenagers are a part of a data-driven generation.
✓ The teenage brain is two times more active than the adult brain and can learn at a faster rate than an adult. Adolescents have more synapses than adults.[13]

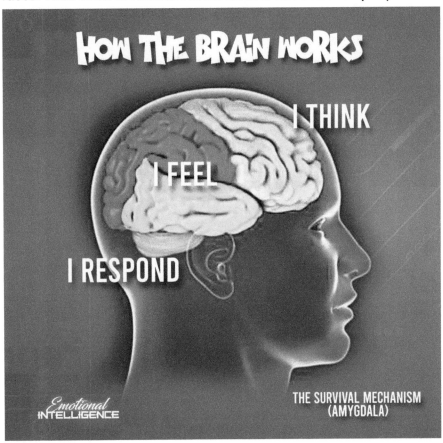

Young Brain's Responses

Adolescents have a brain that is wired with an enhanced capacity for fear and anxiety but is underdeveloped when it comes to calm reasoning. It turns out that the brain circuit for processing fear — the amygdala —which is the smoke detector or the alarm system for the body, is precocious and develops way ahead of the prefrontal cortex control.

What happens when things go wrong: The amygdala, prefrontal cortex, and hippocampus are altered by stress. These parts are often referred as the FRONT MATTERS of the brain.

Amygdala: The amygdala is a small, almond-shaped region of the brain that plays a major role. The **amygdala** is the emotional core for passion, impulse, fear, and aggression. Trauma makes the parts of the brain hypersensitive or renders it insensitive. The amygdala sets off the fight-or-flight response during emotionally triggered situations, reacting to memories or thoughts of dangers.[14]

The over-activity of the amygdala presents as symptoms of hypervigilance and the exaggerated startle response because the amygdala overreacts, norepinephrine is released but then not adequately controlled or dealt with by the prefrontal cortex. As a result, people with high sensitivity to stress or Post Traumatic Stress Disorder (PTSD) experience symptoms of hypervigilance. They become overly aroused and are on high alert, which can make it hard to relax and to sleep. People may feel that they are always tense, and even small triggers can lead them to react as if they are facing or re-experiencing their original trauma (Morey 2012).[15]

FACT ONE: Teens are more impulsive than adults relying less on the prefrontal cortex.
Parietal Lobe is responsible for touch, sight, and language.

FACT TWO: Teens tend to not process information effectively.
Ventral striatum reward center, positive and negative consequence.

FACT THREE: Not fully developed in teens.
The frontal lobe is the house for impulsive behaviors, boredom, excitement, and dramatic changes in mood in the executive human brain functions of the prefrontal cortex:

(Frontal lobe)
- ✓ Shifting and adjusting actions when situations change
- ✓ Foreseeing and weighing possible consequences
- ✓ Understanding impulsivity
- ✓ Forming strategies and planning
- ✓ Organizing thoughts and problem-solving
- ✓ Focusing attention
- ✓ Considering future and predictions
- ✓ Modification of emotions

The executive brain responsible for reasoning is called the **Neocortex**.

Prefrontal Cortex functions include planning and reasoning. Prone to high-risk behaviors in teenagers.

LIMBIC SYSTEM EMOTIONAL BRAIN

THIS ACTS AS AN EARLY WARNING SIGNAL

THE FRONTAL LOBE

THE EXECUTIVE BRAIN, HOUSE FOR IMPULSE BEHAVIORS, BOREDOM, EXCITEMENT AND DRAMATIC CHANGES IN MOOD. CORTEX. RESPONSIBLE FOR REASONING, THINKING, PROBLEM SOLVING, PLANNING.

I THINK RATIONALLY

LIMBIC SYSTEM

HIPPOCAMPUS

HUB MEMORY AND LEARNING. NAVIGATION AND SPATIAL MEMORY, RESPONSIBLE FOR LEARNING, DISTORTED RECALL.

AMYGDALA

THE BRAIN'S ALARM SYSTEM, EMOTIONAL CORE FOR PASSION, IMPULSE, FEAR, AND AGGRESSION, REGULATES BEHAVIORS

Emotional INTELLIGENCE

Limbic System-Emotional brain responsible for emotions

The limbic system remembers information a child associates with a threat (for example, a smell during a difficult situation or clothing similar to that of a violent parent). This association acts as an early warning signal to suggest that a threat is close. The limbic system is a child's built-in sensor.

As therapists, we often use the term "cognitive distortions" to describe irrational, inflated thoughts or beliefs that distort a person's perception of reality, usually in a negative way. Some practitioners believe cognitive distortions can take a severe toll on a child's or adult's mental health during these difficult situations, leading to increased stress, depression, and anxiety. Cognitive distortions can be flawed thinking, often stemming from insecurity and low self-esteem for a child.[16]

I often refer to negative filtering or "Cognitive Schema" as mental flirting, which distorts reality and can generate stressful emotions. "Cognitive schema" is a term that clinical therapists and psychologists use to define how we use little mental shortcuts to organize and to interpret the amounts of stimuli and data that we are experiencing, stirring up thoughts and feelings that produce more negative thoughts. In short, this becomes habitual thinking patterns, since the brain responds to trends. Psychologists call this error thinking.

While working with the educational system, listed below are some distortions that sabotage the classroom.
   1) Mental Flirting
   2) Jumping To Conclusions
   3) Personalization
   4) Black And White Thinking
   5) Catastrophizing
   6) Overgeneralization
   7) Labeling

These **thinking** patterns are classroom-sabotaging and self-defeating, even when it comes from the educator. They occur when the things you are thinking do not match up with reality. Many who repeat the thinking errors don't realize they are doing so.

One of the greatest thinking traps for the classroom is jumping to conclusions. We predict what is going to happen, with little or no evidence. This pattern occurs when there are assumptions made about how a student will behave or respond without any evidence. This leads to trying to interpret another person's thoughts-mind reading. This often lends to power struggles and major communication obstacles.

The amygdala acts as the center for emotions, emotional behaviors, and motivations in the brain. The amygdala is attuned to perceive and recognize a threat and is responsible for triggering the **Fight-Flight** or **Freeze** responses.
In the Reptilian Complex-the survival brain is responsible for instinct.

Hippocampus:

The hippocampus forms and stores episodic memory inside the cerebral cortex. The memories and information is consolidated from short term to long term. In volatile situations the hippocampus stores memories incorrectly and affects memory. In adults, the hippocampus loses neurons with age. During learning the hippocampus provides information to the other brain areas. Without the hippocampus functioning correctly due to cognitive damage, it is impossible to form new memories, and this will create a tremendous learning curve. (Durand. 2019)[17]

The hippocampus is often smaller in people with PTSD or toxic stress and those experiencing trauma. **Youth** with **extreme toxic stress** have abnormal frontolimbic development compared to typically developing young people. The amygdala and hippocampus work together to regulate emotions with a vital responsibility in the survival mode.

People with PTSD or those experiencing toxic stress may experience:
Amygdala-emotion reactions and are overly exaggerated.
The **prefrontal cortex** has dysfunctional thought processes and decision making with inappropriate responses to situations.
Hypothalamus-pituitary-adrenal (HPA) axis-overactive, which leads to an imbalance in hormone levels and increases stress and anxiety. When the brain goes into survival mode, the prefrontal cortex goes offline. In kids who experience severe neglect, the brain is reshaped.

Limbic System acts as the control center for the conscious and the unconscious functions bridging the mind to the body. During stressful encounters the lower brain functions take over.

Survival Mode: Prefrontal

During a stressful situation, the pituitary gland-release-neorohormones-adrenal gland releases adrenaline: causing the brain to function in the **fight**, **flight**, **freeze** response. Below are terms that function during the brain's heighten processing cycle with stress.

Cortisol-shut down the release of neurohormones

When people are in traumatic situations, other areas in the brain shut down.

Anterior cingulate (rational decision making)

Cortex-appears smaller in people with trauma or post-traumatic stress disorder.

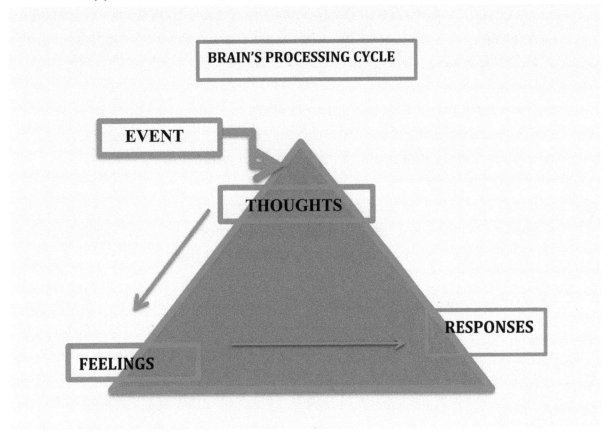

During the brain's processing cycle, students often get in bad moods when the cycle moves toward expressing their feelings. Like most humans, we all get into bad moods. The main reason we have trouble extracting ourselves from our attitude more quickly is that we *cannot* shake a bad feeling, or we are not aware of *what's causing it*, the thoughts behind the mood.

Below are ten common scientific facts that cause bad moods:

1. **Guilt.** Young people can harbor or store guilt from parents, family members, or friends due to past traumatic events. For some, they harbor the blame of parents not being married, and they fantasize about having what they consider a "normal" family. The feeling of even mild guilt can have a significant impact on our mood. Sadly, many of our students struggle with guilt as an issue of social acceptance.

2. **Small rejections**. Rejections are a prevalent emotional injury, especially in the age of social media. Being rejected by peers can lead to devastation. Social psychologist research supports the theory that social identity and being negatively evaluated by others can change the neurological systems within the brain.

3. **Outstanding tasks**. Our mental to-do lists can sit in the back of our minds, nag at us, and bring down our moods. Nevertheless, you do not have to complete *every* outstanding task to improve your mood.

4. **Mental Flirting**. Many of our students can get stuck replaying upsetting scenes that occurred days, weeks, or even months ago. Things that happened in the classroom, on the bus, and even at home.

5. **Low self-esteem.** Dr. Ken Shore says the challenge in working with children with low esteem is to restore belief in themselves. He believes it becomes difficult for a student who harbors low self-esteem. He offers tips: #1 Praise students in a natural and genuine way; #2 Show evidence of progress; #3 Help the student feel important in the class; #4 Help the student deal with adversity.

6. **Fearing failure**. As stated earlier, fearing failure is also closely related to self-worth. Many students put themselves through unbelievable mental torture to avoid failure or to maintain a sense of value. This can cause anxiety or panic.

7. **Feeling disconnected**. Loneliness affects children as well as adults. Our society is driving new levels of alienation and isolation. Disconnection can be quite deadly. We can get so caught up in life we neglect our emotional and social needs and begin to feel disconnected from the people around us.

8. **Getting caught up in small annoyances**. As we go about our busy lives, little annoyances—can place the body in preparation mode for danger further creating anxiety.

9. **Hunger.** This one is pretty obvious, but it is startling how often we forget to consider it. Being hungry impacts our mood. Sudden drops in glucose will impact us far more than we tend to realize. Some students come to school hungry. According to CEO Qiana Thomas of Health Forward Foundation of Kansas City, MO, in her March 13, 2020 Linkedin article During public health crisis, equity should be central solutions, "For millions of our children, school is the one place where they know they will be able to eat."

10. **Exhaustion**. Lack of sleep, exertion until depletion; many of our young students take on adults' responsibilities just to be an added support to their overburdened families. This also falls into the obvious-neglected category.

-The human experience creates loss, challenges, setbacks, and disappointment — therefore trauma do not discriminate.

Chapter Two

TRAUMA

*Trauma (plural traumata) an jury, either physical or psychological
Traumatic neurosis is a neurosis brought on by an extremely painful experience.
Traumatic Stress was discovered after the Vietnam War; however, minority and
oppressed people have had centuries of traumatic experiences.*

Psychological trauma is the emotional response children and young people have to experiencing hostile and distressing situations. According to Dr. Bessel van der Kolk of Boston University Medical Center, traumatic stress became a diagnosis in the wake of the Vietnam War (1965 to 1975), and from there it was applied to other populations experiencing the aftermath of their painful experiences.[18] A child's trauma does not always come from one single identifiable event or life difficulty. Trauma can be the collective impact of adverse experiences in the environment, and with new or old relationships. All trauma impacts the development of a child or a young person. Psychological trauma can result from years of bad mental health, physical health, and stressful experiences.

Types of Traumatic Experiences according to Cognitive Process Theraphy:

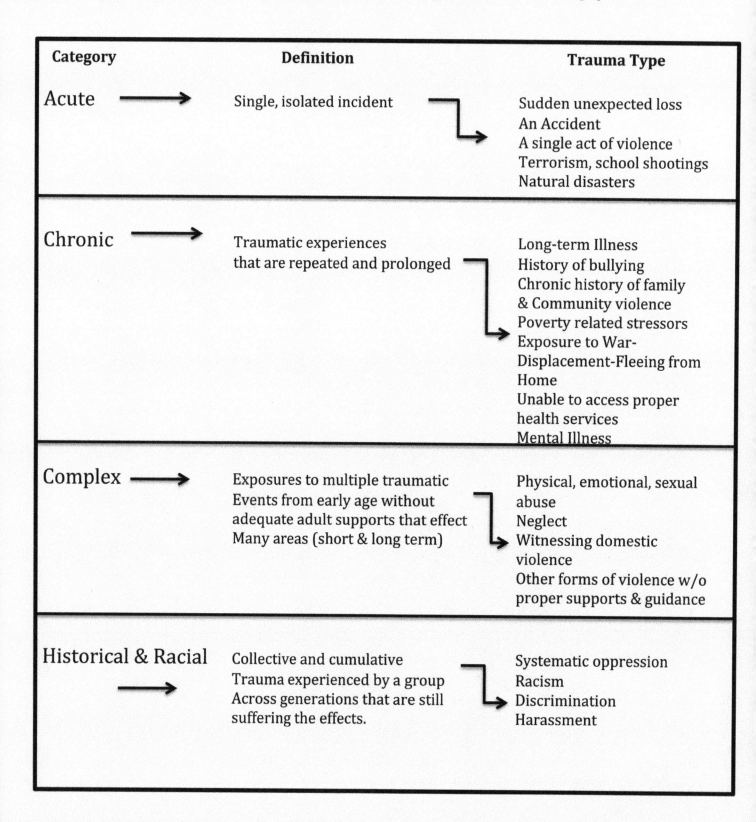

Category	Definition	Trauma Type
Acute	Single, isolated incident	Sudden unexpected loss An Accident A single act of violence Terrorism, school shootings Natural disasters
Chronic	Traumatic experiences that are repeated and prolonged	Long-term Illness History of bullying Chronic history of family & Community violence Poverty related stressors Exposure to War-Displacement-Fleeing from Home Unable to access proper health services Mental Illness
Complex	Exposures to multiple traumatic Events from early age without adequate adult supports that effect Many areas (short & long term)	Physical, emotional, sexual abuse Neglect Witnessing domestic violence Other forms of violence w/o proper supports & guidance
Historical & Racial	Collective and cumulative Trauma experienced by a group Across generations that are still suffering the effects.	Systematic oppression Racism Discrimination Harassment

Psychological Trauma and Mental Health

One out of three adults' mental health conditions are related directly to adverse childhood trauma experiences.[19] Adversity and complex trauma affect the well-being of young people. It increases the risk of mental illness, toxic stress, vulnerable relationships, and issues with the physical health. Mental health can be the hardest subject to talk about, especially when it comes to our children. The mental health community and education have not always fostered healthy connections, however, due to the number of school shootings and systemic racism, educators have been forced to look at the mental health needs of the students and teachers.

Around one in ten young people have a diagnosable mental health condition that translates to three students in every class who experience emotional distress. Mental health problems manifest before the age of fourteen years, as early as age nine, with three to four enduring mental conditions by the age of twenty-four.

Below are seven factors that can lead to emotional distress or an adverse experience.

Mistreatment and Abuse: Childhood abuse, neglect, exposure to substance misuse. Research support that around two in five victims of child exploitation experience mental health problems, including Post Traumatic Stress, and are seventeen times more likely to experience a psychotic episode than peers.

Violence: Exposure to, involvement in, gangs, sexual and domestic violence, or being a child of torture.

Bullying and victimization: including childhood experiences of enduring discrimination, harassment, hate crime, isolation, and prejudice resulting from homophobia, sexism, and racism. 44 percent of these students consider suicide.

Loss and bereavement: including the death of a parent or sibling, involvement in an accident, acquiring an illness or injury, and surviving a natural disaster. Those experiencing loss and bereavement is 1.5 times higher to be diagnose with a mental health condition with a higher risk of depression.

Dis-or-relocation: including complex family breakdown, adopted, or leaving care and being detained in a secure children's service facility; young offenders; homeless; migration. Three in five have some form of emotional and mental health problem.

Adult responsibilities: Caring for adults or siblings in the family and engaging in child labor. Two OUT OF five young caregivers report additional stress relating to the care they provide or lack thereof.

Incarceration of parents or caregivers. According to the Child Wellbeing Study, one in twenty-eight of those young people currently under eighteen years of age have a biological mother or father incarcerated in local jails, state prisons, or federal prison. In urban areas around the US, by age nine, about one-third of all children experience the incarceration of a biological father. This number increases if the child is black or brown.[20]

Most public school districts in America struggle with children and young people from the demographics below:

Demographics of most American Public School Districts in the 21st Century

Racism

Poverty

Drug Use-Abuse- Addiction

Separation of Family

Divorce

Abuse: Sexual, verbal, physical, emotional

Gang influence

Transitional Families

Homelessness

Incarcerated love ones

Children assuming adult roles

Mental illness

Domestic violence

Racism, Privilege, Power

The ugliness of racial oppression, systematic racism, privilege, and explicit silence can affect and lead to chronic stress for children and young adults, placing them within a cycle of emotions that lead to stress. Racism, privilege, and the misuse of power to oppress or the use of explicit or implicit biases can cause trauma for students of color or those marginalized already by society. Racism and privilege hurts and damages black and brown children in real ways. It also hurts their social and emotional health, which has prolonged effects on their mental health. Unconscious attitudes or beliefs about a particular race or gender does affect students. Chronic stress produces changes in their hormones that cause inflammation in the body. The book will provide greater insight into this in the next chapter.

Thoughts from an everyday young adult.

> This past week has been very heavy and also with a full circle of
> emotions. I was 15 when I watched George Zimmerman walk away free
> after murdering Trayvon Martin. I am now witnessing the three latest
> murders of unarmed Black people: Ahmaud Arbery, Breonna Taylor,
> and George Floyd. And I am hurting, just like I was eight years ago, but
> now as an adult and have witnessed no change in this country. I have
> spent all of my K-12 education with predominantly white teachers, and
> I see a lot of silence among my teachers and white peers, and it hurts.
> How should I grieve, or how should I express my anger? You tell me!

Racism is a multi-layered system infused in everything. J. Kehaulani Kauanui
unpacks racism as "a system, not an event" in her 2016 article Settler Colonialism.
Children in households of African Americans, some mixed-race homes, Hispanic and
American Indian populations are more likely to live with higher unemployment and
lower incomes. Persons of color and minorities are less likely to have suitable housing,
proper nutrition, access to good health care, and access to quality education; all due
to the disproportionate rate of the systematic problems in America and socioeconomic factors. Such inequalities increase the risk of health problems. According to
Qiana Thomason, my best girlfriend and CEO of Health Forward Foundation Kansas
City, "As we see in every public health crisis, people of color, particularly African
Americans, have disproportionate rates of infection and mortality due to complex
socioeconomic factors and higher prevalence of underlying conditions."

Spring 2019, I was asked by an eighth grade teacher to speak to her class about the
traumatic impact of the usage of the N- word. The class had become divided because
a small majority of students did not understand the stigma that was associated with
the N- word, and my colleague felted she had exhausted her knowledge base.

The Origin of the N-word

The word "*nigger*" is a key term used in American culture or Western society.
It has been a critical lethal weapon of many of the worst episodes of bigotry in
America's history. It has accompanied uncountable lynchings, beatings, acts of
arson, and other racially motivated attacks upon blacks, people of color, and those
migrating to American soil. It has also been featured in countless jokes and cartoons

that both reflect and encourage the disparagement of blacks and people of color. It is a hurtful racial slur meant to stigmatize mainly African Americans; it is also a weapon against other racial or ethnic groups, including Chinese, Asians, Hispanics, East Indians, Arabs, and darker-skinned people. Discrimination based on skin color is also known as colorism. It is a form of prejudice or discrimination based on the social implications from cultural meanings attached to skin color.

For some blacks, the **N-word** among themselves is a term of **endearment.** Some Black people might say or believe they are entitled to the word, due to the slavery, oppression, racism, and segregation of their ancestors.

The **N-word** is a derogatory term used against Black people. The word originated from the Spanish word "Niger" and "Negro," meaning Black, which describes Black people. The meaning of the word "N" is "an ignorant person." By the late 1800s, particularly during the Trans-Atlantic slave trade, the name was derogatory in manner, and commonly used as a racial slur against Black people. The word "N" has often been used as an insult against people of African descent. The name is hugely offensive and often not mentioned unless one intends to insult another.

According to Randall Kennedy of Harvard, other cultures, many of which have used the N-word against Black people as an attack, now have access to the slang term "Nigga." A person of African descent, let alone someone who is non-Black, whose ancestry doesn't revolve around the sufferings of it, should not speak the word. Some might say they've earned usage of the word because their ancestors died during the middle passage and the Civil Rights Movement when the N-word was used for derogatory purposes only. Whatever the case, this word has no place in the educational classroom or setting.[21]

Other things that affect the young brain:
- Environmental stressors
- Gender
- Economic status
- Role-Functioning
- Support Network
- Individual Habits: sleep, physical activity, substance abuse
- Mental Illness
- Chronic Illness

<u>Cause I ain't got a pencil</u>
By Joshua T. Dickerson

I woke myself
Because we ain't got an alarm clock
Dug in the dirty clothes basket,
Cause ain't nobody washed my uniform
Brushed my hair and teeth in the dark,
Cause the lights ain't on
Even got my baby sister ready
Cause mama wasn't home
Got us both to school on time,
To eat us a good breakfast,
Then when I got to class the teacher fussed at me,
Cause I ain't got a pencil.[22]

What do you KNOW about students with trauma?
Teens who have experienced trauma have less tolerance and exhibit some of the following behaviors:
- Fear
- Inability to trust
- Worry
- Sadness
- Loneliness: feeling alone apart from the other
- Feeling as though people are looking down on them
- Low self-worth
- Increased aggression
- Self-harm
- Defiance and unwillingness to comply with a simple request
- Misplaced emotions
- Truancy
- Low academic scores
- A liking for using jackets and clothing to cover up.
- Being either withdrawn or exhibiting challenging or risky behaviors may be a way that a child communicates emotional distress and attempts to make sense of the adversity.

Everyday Students with trauma experiences

Shaking the bottle before it explodes. Most days,' children who live with trauma bottles are shaken before they arrive or load the bus before getting to the schoolyard. Often the pressure is a result of an **adult's responsibility** or **response.**

For example, Veronica arrives home and finds the lights are shut off. Not to mention her English and Social Studies class assignments are due the next day. Both tasks require usage of electricity and Wi-Fi connection. Mom becomes more stressed in addition to her boyfriend, who recently moved in but was released from his job because he lied on a job application, not disclosing he is a felon. Now boyfriend yells at Veronica, creating a highly emotional atmosphere for a physical altercation between mom and him.

Or other scenarios such as grandma, who is the primary caretaker because mom is a recovering addict and dad has moved to Atlanta, with his new girlfriend. Grandma is rushed to the hospital, no food in the refrigerator, the washing machine is not working, and the 6th-grade middle school student has to wear the same clothes to school. He wears his coat every day to hide the fact that it is the same outfit. The student lives in a heavily policed neighborhood, bullied, the dread of gang violence, and so on. This student goes through war to enter the schoolyard. So, when the educator says, Good Morning, the student yells at the teacher instead and says "the F-bomb" The student is sent to the office for the use of profanity because the teacher has no idea what day the student faced.

EVERYDAY STUDENTS' EXPERIENCES
- Intrusive thoughts, feelings
- Traumatic dreams
- Flashbacks
- Intense psychological distress triggered by reminders of old memories
- Physiological reactivity

EXPERIENCE INCREASED AROUSAL
- Sleep difficulty
- Irritability, assaultive behavior
- Difficulty concentrating
- Difficulty remembering
- Hypervigilance
- Startle response

TEACHERS SEE PERSISTENT AVOIDANCE
- Of thoughts, feelings, talking of activities, places, people associated with trauma
- Inability to recall
- Numbness, detachment, estrangement
- Restricted affect
- Foreshortened future

According to Dr. Richard Curwin, the more adverse experience-traumatized children have an underdeveloped frontal lobe and overdeveloped fight or flight reflex. That combination makes it extremely difficult to stay composed when stressed and on-task in class.[23]

Effective Tools for building relationship with young people
Connecting

Slowing down

Understand

Gentle touch sometimes

Supporting

The Power of Words

Perception research confirms that life's successes and failures link to personal perception attitudes about self-worth.[24] When I worked as an addiction counselor in 1997, I had a slogan that I often repeated: "Where the mind goes the behind will follow."

According to Andrew Newberg, MD, and Mark Robert Waldman, words can change your brain. In their book, *Words Can Change Your Brain*, they write: "a single word has the power to influence the expression of genes that regulate physical and emotional stress."[25]

Positive words alter the expression of genes, strengthening areas in the frontal lobes, and promoting the brain's cognitive functioning. They propel the motivational centers of the brain into action, according to the authors, and build resiliency.

Hostile words during traumatic experiences can disrupt specific genes that play a crucial part in the production of neurochemicals that protect us from stress. Humans are hardwired for fear and worry—due to our brains protecting us from threats to our survival. "Angry words send alarm messages through the brain, and they partially shut down the logic-and-reasoning centers located in the frontal lobes," writes Newberg and Waldman.

A single negative word can increase activity in the amygdala. This releases dozens of stress-producing hormones and neurotransmitters, which in turn interrupt our brains' functioning. This happens when people are overly criticized and exposed to emotional trauma or emotional abuse.

According to the authors, using the right words can transform our reality:

> By holding a positive and optimistic [word] in your mind, you stimulate frontal lobe activity. This area includes specific language centers that connect directly to the motor cortex responsible for moving you into action. And as our research has shown, the longer you concentrate on positive words, the more you begin to affect other areas of the brain. Functions in the parietal lobe start to change, which changes your perception of yourself and the people you encounter daily. A positive view of yourself will bias you toward seeing the good in others, whereas a negative self-image will include you toward suspicion and doubt. Over time the structure of your thalamus will also change in response to your conscious words, thoughts, and feelings, and we believe that the thalamic changes affect how you perceive reality.[26]

When students are always overly criticized, verbally, or emotionally abused, insulted, treated disrespectfully, and neglected, these messages say they are worthless, and these young people set up life situations that support that view.[27] When people are upset, the ability to put things into words disappears.

Rapper Smoke D of UGK, "Growing up, I became accustomed to physical whoppings, because my caretaker taught me I would be a better person if I got whoppings for the things that I would do in the future, so I got whoppings every day whether I have deserved it or not. After a while, the whoppings became ineffective. They did not hurt. I had conditioned myself to get whoppings. Once my caretaker saw that I was numb to the whoppings, she began to use literal words to whop me. So I began to hear things like, "*I wish you were never born.*" The more words spoke on me, the more unpredictable and destructive I became, which lead me to a life of crime, becoming physical and emotionally abusive."[28]

Teachers, parents, friends, pastors, and coaches are self-concept builders for teens and children.[29] Teachers can help students learn assertive techniques and problem solving and critical thinking strategies. The individual with a high self-concept is motivated, self-assured, cognitively aware, and responsible for his or her behavior. Since self-concept is learned and not inherited, so it can be changed.

Harsh criticism can destroy people rather than help!

SUPPORTING STUDENTS WITH TRAUMA
Two types of students:

Regulated students are those who can **regulate normal** emotions. Regulated students have all five areas met. Regulation is the ability to experience and maintain stress within one's window of tolerance: being calm, focused, and relaxed.
Dysregulation: the student who experiences stress outside of one's window of tolerance, stressed out in a state of distress.[30]

DYSREGULATED STUDENTS	REGULATED STUDENTS
Hyper-arousal	Responsive
Unable to Focus	Engaged
Cannot Adhere to Expectations	Focused
Aggressive Verbally and Physically	Calm
Resistant to Directives	Uses words to express feelings

Argumentative	Willing to comply with instructions
Anxious	Can regulate and self-soothe in difficulty
Impulsive	Understands boundaries
Struggles to remember	Self-Aware
Defiant	Self-Motivated
Withdrawn	Uses Social Skills
Tardy	Critically Thinks
Chronic Absence	Solve Problems or Dilemmas
Shut down	Can and will ask for help
Avoids task	Opened to listen and understand
Numbs Out	Accountable for actions

Terms Every Educator Needs To Know

Triggers: refers to critical factors that cause the emotional onsets within our students. What are your students' emotional triggers?

Reset: Means to de-escalate or start over emotionally. What is needed for your student to restart or reset emotionally? Do they need an emotional break or a sip of water?

Calming room/corner: a designated room or classroom space for students to reset. What space in your classroom is designed for your students to reset?

Student Behavioral Contract: agreement with student and teacher concerning target behaviors. What agreements can you and your student form regarding practices and actions?

TRAUMA AND ATTACHMENTS

Children with trauma can develop what as therapists we call *trauma bonding* or *attachment disorder*. They might experience other attachment problems having difficulty connecting to others and managing their own emotions. This results in a lack of trust and self-worth, a fear of getting close to anyone, anger, and a need to be in control. A child with an attachment disorder feels unsafe and alone.

Attachment disorders are the result of negative experiences in beginning formative relationships. If young children feel repeatedly abandoned, isolated, powerless, or uncared for—for whatever reason—**they will learn that they can't depend on others, and the world is a dangerous and frightening place**.

So why do some children develop attachment disorders while others don't? The answer has to do with the attachment process, which relies on the interaction of parent, child, and surroundings.

Attachment disorder and other attachment problems occur when children have been unable to connect with a parent or primary caregiver consistently. This inability can happen for many reasons:

1. A baby cries and no one responds or offers comfort.
2. A baby is hungry or wet, and ignored for hours.
3. No one looks at, talks to, or smiles at the baby, so the baby feels alone.
4. A young child gets attention only by acting out or displaying other extreme behaviors.
5. A young child or baby is mistreated or abused.
6. Sometimes the child's needs are met, and sometimes they aren't. The child never knows what to expect.
7. The infant or young child is hospitalized or separated from his or her parents.
8. A baby or young child is moved from one caregiver to another (can be the result of adoption, foster care, or the loss of a parent).
9. The parent is emotionally unavailable because of depression, an illness, or a substance abuse problem.

As the examples show, sometimes the circumstances that cause the attachment problems are **unavoidable**, but the child is too young to understand what has happened and why. To a young child, it just feels like no one cares, and they lose trust in others, and the world becomes an unsafe place.

Early warning signs and symptoms of insecure attachment:

1. Avoids eye contact
2. Does not smile
3. Does not reach out to be picked up
4. Rejects your efforts to calm, soothe, and connect
5. Does not seem to notice or care when you leave them alone
6. Cries inconsolably
7. Does not follow you with his or her eyes
8. Is not interested in playing interactive games or playing with toys
9. Spends a lot of time comforting themselves

It's important to note that the early symptoms of insecure attachment are similar to the first symptoms of other issues, such as ADHD and autism.

Everyday children need **Validating-Accepting-Engaging-Apologizing.**

HER STORY, age 14

When I was four years old, my mama went to prison for seven years. I had to live with my granny the whole time. Throughout the time my mom was in prison, my grandma struggled to care for the three of us because she has cancer and she was sick. When my mama finally came home in 2018, she didn't get us nor did she want us. She just ran the streets because she was back to her old life of using drugs. She also got pregnant with my little brother Nasir. Mom was still using drugs when my brother was born. He was a healthy baby, and then two months later he passed away. My family says it wasn't because of her using drugs. When she was pregnant, they say it was something calls SIDS, which stand for sudden infant death! Ever since that day my life has been a mess. It's hard for me to trust adults now, even those in my family, because they are always screwing things up for us.

HIGHLY ENGAGED AND PARTICIPATING.
SEES ONE-SELF AS A VALUED MEMBER
TO INSPIRE AND HELP OTHERS.

SELF - ACTUALIZATION

ENGAGED. I AM
IMPORTANT

ESTEEM

I AM ALMOST ENGAGED BUT
THERE ARE TIMES I AM NOT

LOVE/BELONGING

NOT ENGAGED OR
MOTIVATED AT ALL

SAFETY & SECURITY

I AM HERE ONLY BECAUSE
IT IS REQUIRED (I HAVE TO BE)

**PHYSIOLOGICAL
& SURVIVAL**

Emotional
INTELLIGENCE

Exposure to trauma can affect many areas of one's life and can increase the risk of a range of vulnerabilities, according Dr. Kathleen Young, clinical psychologist specializing in the treatment of trauma and its aftermath.[31]

- ✓ **Physiological Needs** must be addressed first. (Homeostasis regulated, rested, freedom from hunger, clothing, and etc.; basic needs met).
- ✓ **Safety**: physically safe, emotionally safe (student must trust that teachers want their best interest), freedom from bullying and intimidation, freedom from harsh punishment by the teacher or to be penalized when teacher is upset.
- ✓ **Relationships/Love:** From friends; teachers, school administration, counselors, school personnel, and family: **In urban school settings, relationships are vital;** they are the catalyst to success. Teachers must like their students.
- ✓ **Esteem:** self-esteem, self-respect, confidence, respect of others, desire to achieve.

- *Relationship Problems* – difficulty with communication, trouble setting or maintaining healthy boundaries, repeating unhealthy patterns in relationships, trouble choosing safe partners, difficulty getting close to people, difficulty trusting others, or falling into abusive patterns with others.

- *Social Alienation* – feeling alone, feeling different from others, never feeling accepted, feeling stigmatized, and/or experiencing social phobia.

- *Low Self-Esteem* – self-doubt, self-blame, shame, feeling like a "bad" person, and/or feeling like an imposter.

- *Difficulty Thinking*– dissociation, "spacing out," feel confused, difficulty interpreting the world accurately, amnesia or forgetting parts of your life, and/or trouble concentrating.

- *Difficulty with Feelings* –difficulty recognizing, managing, or "appropriately" expressing feelings, depression, panic attacks, anxiety, problems with anger, disruptive fear(s), substance dependency or abuse, nightmares, and/or self-harm behaviors.

- *Body Issues* – disconnection or dissociation from one's body, a feeling of being "unreal," distorted body image, harsh judgment or hatred of the body or body parts, self-harm behaviors, eating disorders, substance dependence or abuse, sexual problems, and/or numbing of bodily areas.

- *Sexual Challenges* – sexual inhibition or compulsive sexual behavior, flashbacks to abusive experiences during sexual contact, inability to achieve orgasm, pain, or numbing during intimacy, and/or sexual aggression towards others.

- *Physical problems* – persistent body aches (chronic pain), physical issues that arise when stressed, digestive issues (stomach aches, vomiting, irritable bowel syndrome), backaches, migraines, arthritis, chronic fatigue, feeling agitated or physically restless, and/or sexual problems.

Trauma can impact your relationships and personal health, adding stress to your body. It can cause:

- Fibromyalgia
- Autoimmune Diseases
- Migraine Headaches

Trauma plays a major role in many mental health disorders:

- Trauma-related Anxiety
- Trauma and Substance Abuse
- Trauma and Borderline Personality Disorder
- Dissociative Disorders
- Trauma–related Eating Disorders

Trauma impacts your relationships:

- Relationships after Severe Trauma vs Making Healthy Choices
- Family of Choice
- Forgiveness and Trauma: Are Some Things Unforgivable?[32]

Trauma Reaction Scenarios in Children

- "A" students become "C" students; severe reactions cause others to fail altogether. **Cognitive dysfunction involving memory and learning.**
- One boy witnessed his father being killed trying to cross the border with his parents when he was six years old. Now he is thirteen years old. He still sleeps on the floor, ever ready to run from danger, and experiences hypervigilant responses at school with **tremendous fear and anxiety.**
- The twins live with domestic violence. Revenge is a constant theme at their home when the incident has been a violent one. At school, the teachers see increased aggression, fighting, assaultive behavior – these are their first responses.
- The student walks home every day with two other students from the neighborhood. At the time of a random drive-by shooting, a fellow student feels a form **of survivor guilt.**
- I met an eleven-year-old young man one year after his sister had been shot to death as bullets invaded their home. He still has dreams at home, so he is afraid of falling to sleep, so he sleeps in his first period English language arts class. **Traumatic Dreams.**

OVERVIEW

Trauma Children may exhibit the following behaviors:

- Trouble sleeping, being afraid to sleep alone even for short periods.
- Be easily startled (terrorized) by sounds, sights, smells similar to those that existed at the time of the event – a car backfiring may sound like the gunshot that killed someone; for one child, his dog pouncing down the stairs brought back the sound of his father falling down the stairs and dying.
- Become hypervigilant – forever watching out for and anticipating that they are about to be or are in danger.
- Seek safety "spots" in their environment, in whatever room they may be in at the time. Children who sleep on the floor instead of their bed after a trauma do so because they fear the comfort of a bed will let them sleep so hard that they won't hear danger coming.
- Become irritable, aggressive, act tough, provoke fights.
- Verbalize a desire for revenge.
- Act as if they are no longer afraid of anything or anyone, verbalizing that nothing ever scares them anymore, and in the face of danger, respond inappropriately.
- Forget recently acquired skills.
- Return to behaviors they had previously stopped; i.e., bed-wetting, nail-biting, or developing disturbing behaviors such as stuttering.
- Withdraw and want to do less with their friends.
- Develop physical complaints: headaches, stomach problems, fatigue, and other ailments not previously present.
- Become accident-prone, taking risks they had previously avoided, putting themselves in life-threatening situations, reenacting the event as a victim or a hero.
- Develop a pessimistic view of the future, losing their resilience to overcome additional difficulties, losing hope, losing their passion to survive, play, and enjoy life.

A child's brain is highly responsive to the threat of stress in their environment.

 Brief increases in heart rate,
mild elevations in stress hormone levels.

 Serious, temporary stress responses,
buffered by supportive relationships.

Prolonged activation of stress
response systems in the absence
of protective relationships.

Chapter Three
STRESS METER

A recent study from the Center on the Developing Child at Harvard University indicates that trauma, along with toxic stress, can permanently change a child's body and brain, resulting in severe lifelong complications.[33]

When faced with stress, our body prepares to respond by increased heart rate, blood pressure, muscle tension, and breathing, and releasing cortisol and adrenaline. When a child experiences stress, their executive functions are knocked offline, and the child goes into self-preservation or survival mode. This means that they spend a significant amount of time in a state of hyperarousal, facing significant emotional distress. This is the effect of dysregulation. It causes them to find it challenging to calm themselves and return to a window of tolerance or a place of calm. Stress may prevent a child from learning and having healthy teacher-student relationships, and creates long-term health problems. Cortisol and norepinephrine are two neurochemical systems that are critical in the stress response.

For children, toxic stress can overload their developmental system and change their hormone levels.

Stress can create a hormone level change for a young person. This can cause a drastic impact on brain structure and function, as well as other organs in the body, thus producing lifelong physical and mental health problems. High levels of **cortisol** and **adrenaline** will keep the blood pressure elevated, which causes a weak heart and circulatory system. High levels of these hormones can lead to type 2 diabetes or even disrupt the immune system, which will make their body prone to other illnesses, such as depression, lupus, and abdominal obesity, and reduce the ability to fight off infections such as the common cold.

Trauma is linked to thymus involution, which **impairs immunity and increases inflammation.**

Stress reduces the child's ability to learn and or figure out things, which will result in behavioral symptoms displayed in the classroom. Toxic and environmental stress can harm a child's brain. A lower window of tolerance in students can result in behaviors such as fighting, checking out, eloping, truancy, and defiance with verbal disrespect. This also creates difficulty in making friends and maintaining positive relationships. (Center for Developing Child: Harvard University)[34]

Looking at stress through a neurological lens, we are born with billions of neuron and brain nerve cells. These are the connections between our vision, hearing, language, and cognitive functioning. The frequent activation of the two stress hormones (**cortisol** and **adrenaline**) can reduce the neural connection for the executive thinking area, which will limit a child's cognitive abilities. Harvard studies suggest continual trauma will weaken the neural pathways, **bypassing thinking, and strengthening the survival mode of functioning, making a child less incapable of coping with difficulty and adversity.**

This creates **hypervigilance,** in which young people are continually looking to identify and detect a threat.

When students experience stressors, their reptilian brain experiences an emotional hijacking (giving energy or draining energy), activating the fight-flight-freeze response, which causes them to focus on the small picture or small matters, which govern fear and anger.

When this happens, the student:
1. Resists change
2. Retreats to familiar
3. Needs structure

This can shut down the rest of the brain and body.

A newer study by Harvard suggests that stress may have **epigenetic changes.** Dr. John Launer believes a trauma-exposed stress environment can develop your genetic capacity or alter which gene to turn on or off referring to gene modification. "Trauma can induce epigenetic changes for genes related to mental health, obesity, drug addiction, immune function, metabolic disease, and heart disease."[35]

The Importance of Sleep and Stress in Children and Young People

- Stress arises in a teenager when there is sleep deprivation. The sleep process releases melatonin. Teenagers' brains do not release melatonin until 1 am. Adults release melatonin at 10 or 11 pm. Teenagers' brains are more sensitive to stress than adults.

- Sleep is an essential way in which we restore ourselves, and that process of restoration that occurs during REM sleep. Dream sleep is an important factor in the way traumatic memories don't get integrated.

- Sleep helps consolidate memory and learning. Chronic sleep deprivation contributes to a delay integrating the day's learning experiences and the ability to recall information.

- Stress can impair learning.

- Students' awards systems are high, focusing on minor things that become major for them. The virtual world also creates stress in students.

- Teenage boys' brains show that boys take more risk than girls.

- Due to boys' risky behaviors, boys' peak and emergence into mental illness happens faster than girls. Significant signs of mental illness can be seen as early as age twelve in boys.

Addiction and Substance Abuse

Many trauma survivors also encounter substance abuse issues, as they attempt to self-medicate from the harmful effects of trauma and stress.

The teenage brain is more susceptible to injury. Addiction and substance abuse last longer in teenagers, and teenagers get addicted faster. Twelve-to-nineteen-year-olds have a heightened risk for substances.

- ✓ Alcohol blocks the plasticity of the teenage brain and stops the memory.
- ✓ Binge drinking can cause brain damage easily in the adolescent.

✓ Marijuana and inhalants can cause functional impairment with recalling memory, but they discontinue the memory staying in the brain for up to four days, causing the student to lose concentration and focus.

✓ Marijuana use can cause the development of anxiety in the adolescent.

✓ Marijuana can contribute to the onset of other mental illnesses in adolescents. Marijuana can trigger the onset of psychosis, schizophrenia, anxiety, and depression in the adolescent years.

According to the Institute for Substance Abuse Treatment Evaluation, opioids work by attaching to proteins in the brain, spinal cord, and gastrointestinal tract, called opioid receptors. When opioids attach to opioid receptors, they block the transmission of pain messages to the brain, resulting in a person feeling little to no pain. Opioids induce a euphoric feeling to form in a user's body by affecting the brain regions that mediate pleasure. People who abuse opioids commonly feel pleasurable, warm, and drowsy, as well as at ease with all matters in their lives. Opioid abuse relieves stress in people because the drugs are sedatives and will detach a person from pain or doing any strenuous activities. Besides, opioids will reduce a user's heart rate, cause constipation, cause a widening of blood vessels, and depress coughing and breathing reflexes.[36]

With mentioning again, the presence of stability can regulate these changes in the early years and help children cope better with adversity when they grow up instead of using marijuana and inhalants.

By the time a student enters middle school, they have already dealt with a cycle of emotions. If left unchecked, these cycles of emotions can lead to depression and or anxiety.

Chapter Four

THE DISPLAY OF EMOTIONS

In this chapter, you will identify the benefits of understanding trauma and the display of emotions in young people. When you know what to expect, it becomes much easier to manage them.

Students of every sphere and grade level experience their share of trauma and display the emotions within the academic setting. For most students, trauma occurs at the hands of people who are supposed to take care of them. With this nature of pain, the brain sometimes does not allow a story to create; however, the images, the sounds, and physical sensations don't change over time. So these students need additional support in the educational setting.

An emotionally intelligent educator transforms his or her *classroom*. The educator is equipped and empowered with tools to understand the trauma of his/her students, while helping them achieve maximum academic success. An emotionally intelligent school identifies all triggers of negativity, assisting students in coping in more positive manners. By understanding one's feelings, the educator can understand and evaluate students in the areas below.

Self-Awareness, Self-Regulation, Social Skills, and **Self-Motivation**
Paul Ekman in, 1970, identified six universal components of emotions. Educators experience at least all six emotions from at least thirty different student personalities in a given day.

Happiness-Surprise-Sadness-Anger-Disgust-Fear
The mystery to the display of emotions is that social constructs are the factors of how they will be displayed.
Every school-aged learner experiences transitions.

DEAR TEACHERS,

*Next **WEDNESDAY**, when those sweet faces show up for the first day, and you are excited to give the familiar opener, "How was your summer and What did you do during the summer?" please consider the kid whose family couldn't afford a vacation after the reopening of the economy or the recent stay at home order due to COVID-19. The student who took care of younger siblings because their grown-ups slept all day — the student who hid under the covers during morning hours, trying to escape the screaming and cursing. The ones looking forward to lunch because they've only had the same sandwich all summer or haven't been fed at all and have spent their summer looking for ways to feed him/herself and his/her siblings. The kid who is wearing last's year's clothes because his/her family could not afford new ones. Sadly, many students are dreading the first day of school because they have no right answers for what they did this summer when what they did was **survive**.*

*So please consider a different question. Perhaps, "What are you looking forward to about this school year?" And please don't make them go around the room writing or telling about their summer. **Sadly, for a lot of kids, the best part is that summer is over.***

<u>**Transition:**</u> always comes with a lot of questions.
- ➤ Who am I?
- ➤ How do I fit in or belong?
- ➤ How do I understand this new challenge?
- ➤ What do others think about me?
- ➤ How different am I from my siblings or others?
- ➤ How different am I from my parents?

Understanding the Mood Swings

Mood swings are frequent in young people and teenagers, with them being happy sometimes and cranky other times. Anything and everything can set them off, and they can go on endless tirades of how unfair you are.

Mood swings can also indicate depression sometimes. Parents and teachers sometimes cannot distinguish between teen rebellion and mood swings. The duration of the mood swings and the severity of the mood swing should be considered.

Aggression

Teenagers may get angry with you often and for unclear reasons. They may become argumentative and talk back more. Understand that anger is a normal human emotion, and it is common among teens. But if they don't channel their anger correctly, it can become aggression and result in violence, which can be dangerous to them and others.

Solution:

A common mistake that parents and teachers make is underestimating what the student is going through. **Parents,** you may feel that your child is overreacting, but that will only make them feel misunderstood. That can shut them off completely. Avoid giving advice or diverting the topic. Rather than brushing off their reaction, try to listen and empathize. Let them talk about it, and you may even be able to lead them to realize that the drama is not worth it.[37]

During these transitions or cycles of emotions, all students need an intentional space.

Every school classroom needs intentional space. Create intentional space to talk to your student or child about what's going on: *body changes, friendships, emotions, self-explorations, external pressures, and how they are having fun.* **This is essential for all parents, caregivers, and guardians of a middle school student or a new freshman.**

Create a network of safe outlets where a child can have fun, as well as develop social skills such as **trust**, **friendships**, **independence**, **respect**, **responsibility**, **and healthy habits,** and improve their unique gifts and graces.

What you hear is essential. Learn code words and learn body language

What do students need at school to make learning better?

Build and develop a healthy, secure relationship vs. coddling a student. Please do not coddle students as a form of building a relationship. Coddling is when an educator lowers the academic expectations for students, or when implicit biases weigh in thinking and teachers generalize to a fault.

- ✓ Regulate activities in the classroom to calm the brain and increase the window of stress tolerance.
- ✓ Help students with transitions (halls, cafeteria). Many students are stressed out about transitions especially, those entering middle school or high school as first timers.
- ✓ Create a regulating learning environment. Some educational spaces/classrooms are too busy and overstimulating by hanging too many items from the ceiling. Use soft, warm colors, and warm lighting

Observation from a Trauma-Informed Elementary Principal:

Hanging too much stuff from ceilings can create overstimulation or wondering, having too many subjects in the same space can be confusing for a learner, moving the To Do/Agenda around each week can create confusion, Not having a calendar or schedule illustrates low expectations. I find that space in classrooms, congestion, and poorly organized spaces is also frustrating to students.

Principal Stacie Wadlington — Saint Louis.

I have also learned that assigning seats in elementary school is less traumatic for students than allowing them to pick their own.

Relationship-Based Formula:

1. The teacher connects with the student, building a relationship. A teacher must be emotionally healthy.
2. When the connection is established, teachers can help a dysregulated student instead of sending them out. Teachers should teach critical thinking, stress techniques, meditation, and coping in the classroom.
3. The student can self-regulate when there is a greater sense of emotional awareness.

How do I get the student to change this behavior (dysregulated behaviors)? Find out what are the physiological, safety, relationship, and esteem needs to decrease stress. Teachers are a not therapists; however, a teacher can be a good investigator. Remember: **A student dysregulated will not perform academically.**

Proactive Strategies
- ✓ Create a Family Culture in your Class (you matter)
- ✓ Address Development Deficits Immediately
- ✓ Learn to use Movement in the Classroom
- ✓ Keep the Classroom Safe: Safe from Bullying and Intimidation, and Teachers use your discretionary space and moments.
- ✓ Make School Fun

DISPLAY OF EMOTIONS AT SCHOOL
Emotional Responses in Elementary and Middle School

Please Note: When a student has reached this point they hear little in regards to consequences.

Warning Emotions Displayed in Elementary and Middle School

Frustration	Risky Behavior	Mild Aggression	Irritable
Discouraged	Continual Tapping	Irritable	Climbing on objects
Hyper	Afraid-Suspicious	Overly Silly	Pacing
Fidgety	Fear	Jumpy	Overly Energetic

Warning Emotions: Today is not a good: on the road toward dysregulation.

Sadness	Moving Slowly	Sleepy	Feeling trapped
Sick	Carelessness	Unable to communicate verbally	Nonverbal communication is short

Dysregulated Emotions that may need a Student Referral, Phone call home, and Administrative Actions.

Anger	Mad and unable to self-soothe	Out of Control	Using objects to harm self or others
Yelling	Elated beyond calm	Elopes	Sitting under a table

Physical and verbal Aggression	Throwing Items	Unresponsive	Obscene gestures
Bullying	Annoyed	Repeated insubordination	Written threats

What hinders positive emotional responses?

Negative experiences, anger, sadness, inability to trust friends and peers, and yelling.

What are at least three ways you can express yourself positively and healthy?

- ➢ Use your words and do not be disrespectful
- ➢ Have a healthy face
- ➢ Be polite

The Emotional Intelligent Student/ Regulated

Calm	Focused	Open to Communicate	Ready to Learn
Kind	Happy and Okay	Prepared	Responsive
Resolves Conflict	Friendly-Respectful	Follows Simple Instructions	Cooperative
Safe	Responsible for Choices	Kind	Excited without major disruptions

Teachers, please be aware of this: Know your students

- ✓ Cognitive development
- ✓ Language development
- ✓ Academic development
- ✓ Social development
- ✓ Physical development
- ✓ Emotional development

Traditional Views in School

- ✓ Extreme consequences that do not fit the incident and overly exaggerated written referrals
- ✓ Rewards and incentives create motivation; stickers, food, and extra time

✓ External control (points, charts, detentions, and removal of privileges)
✓ Time-out
✓ Behavioral management
✓ Performance outcomes
✓ Interventions
✓ The student to fit the environment
✓ Behavior is a matter of choice.

Best Practice Model

✓ Relational influence creates motivation for learning
✓ Internal control (sense of self of accomplishments, self-acceptance)
✓ Time-in vs time-out
✓ Expectations based on emotional social age
✓ Stress management
✓ Community family focus
✓ Process-based interventions
✓ Proactive prevention
✓ All transitions Identified
✓ Environments to fit the student

(E) EMOTIONS ACTIVITY FOR STUDENTS

Explosive Anger

1. There is some good in the worst of us and some evil in the best of us. When we discover this, we are less prone to hate our enemies . . . Someone must have sense enough and morality enough to cut off the chain of hate.

2. Physical Response to anger:
Anger increases the risk of headache, heart races –heart attacks, becoming drowsy: experiencing emotional shutdown; stress that can lead to stroke, and other cardiovascular problems.

3.Understanding Anger
People with anger issues *tend to misunderstand* other people's intentions. We must learn not to always accuse others. A libeler is one who falsely and maliciously accuses a person.

QTIP=Quit taking it personally

Excuse people rather than accuse people

4. Do not be confrontational when you are angry.
They think others are being hostile (even when they are not) and make the wrong conclusions about others' intentions.

5. Drop the judgment of yourself and others: **Endorse yourself**. You don't look to others to control you.

6. Don't let your outer environment affect your internal or inner environment.

7. I can't control other people with my anger. You are only responsible for your emotional responses and actions.

Strategies

8. Stop — Think before you speak. Use an outlet

- ➤ Once you're calm, express your **anger** in verbal or written form without doing harm
- ➤ Exercise
- ➤ Listen to music
- ➤ Take a time-out. ...
- ➤ Identify possible solutions. ...
- ➤ Stick with 'I' statements. ... QTIP: Quit taking it personally
- ➤ Don't hold a grudge. ...
- ➤ Use humor to release tension
- ➤ Choose your reactions

(E) EMOTIONS ACTIVITY
FOR TEACHERS AND PARENTS

1. What happens to people when they remember bad stuff?

2. What happens to people who live in pain, aggressiveness, and danger? What are the names given to ethnic groups?

3. What are the effects on the brain of not reading or writing, not having a good education?

4. Why is the family so important? Who is in your family? How does the system of oppression split up the family?

5. How do we disrespect each other: emotionally and physically?

6. Why do students try to impress others? Give me an example of a time when a student tried to impress someone.

7. Pick a student who was gunned down. Create four slides about them.

(E) EMOTIONS ACTIVITIES FOR PARENTS

Your child is discovering themselves outside of their last name or their ethnic group. You, as a parent, are also learning your child in a new way.

Independence:
- ❖ Develop study habits
- ❖ Get familiar with the latest technology, fades, music,
- ❖ Know what is entering the minds and ears of your child.
- ❖ Instagram..Facebook (thirteen years) ...Twitter...Google alert...YouTube... Wi-Fi restrictions
- ❖ Get familiar with video games. Ex: **Grand Theft Auto, Fortnite**
- ❖ Middle school language*: ex: Thot*
- ❖ Cellphone passwords

What you hear is essential. Learn code words and learn body language with middle school students.
- ➢ Help your student learn healthy problem-solving techniques
- ➢ Help your student learn healthy conflict-resolution skills
- ➢ Help your student develop trust
- ➢ Help your student learn the difference between realistic and unrealistic expectations.

Show your child that no matter how much you work, you are interested and involved.
- ➢ Get to know your child's friends.
- ➢ Get to know your child's body language. What does sadness look like for your middle school student? What does happiness look like?
- ➢ What is your child's love?
- ➢ What new patterns has your child picked up since attending middle school?

Discuss uncomfortable topics
Sex, drugs, strangers, peer pressure, bullying, STDs.

PICTURES FROM AN EMOTIONAL INTELLIGENT LEARNING SPACE-STL
(Science-7th grade, Mrs. Drummond)

Decorative Light Covers by **Octolights** used in a Social-Emotional Classroom.
www.decorativelightcovers.com

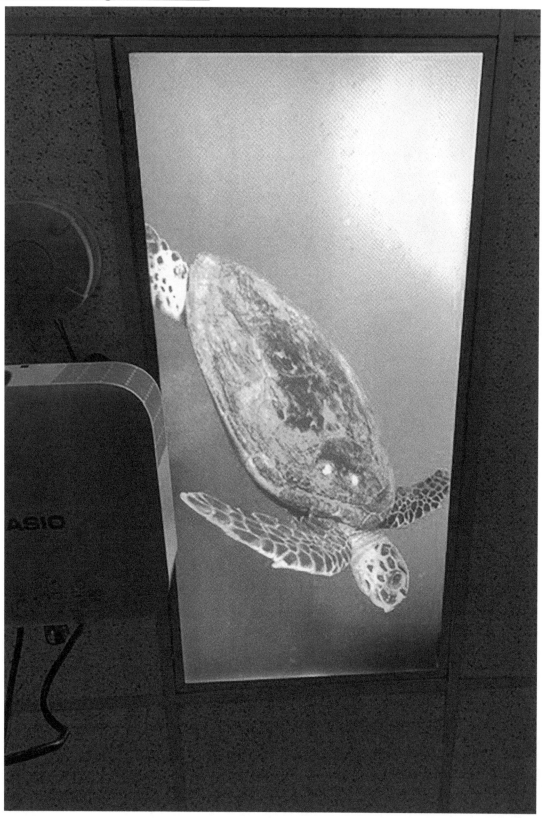

Decorative Light Covers by *Octolights* used in a Social-Emotional Classroom.
www.decorativelightcovers.com

Schools are, therefore, places where "children and adolescents learn to reach beyond early conceptualizations of the family trust to initiate trusting relationships with classmates and teachers" (Ennis & McCauley, 2002, p. 15)

Chapter Five
CHANGING THE CLIMATE IN THE CLASSROOM

Same instruction-regardless of race, bias, gender, social economics, experiences.

"Teaching can have very powerful amazing effects,"
said Loewenberg Ball. "It can also do incredible damage."

When creating classroom climate changes that are conducive to trust and cooperative learning, the educator requires both skill and motivation. When dealing with disruptive and disengaged students, the educator can demonstrate their trust by encouraging students to be responsible for classroom target goals and individual behavior, and by giving students second chances to behave appropriately and connect with the teacher in the classroom. Trust has to be facilitated and reinforced with other attributes. **If I trust you, I can respect you.**

Students and educators are together in a classroom for up to 188 days of the year: there should be evidence of creativity, flexibility, responsiveness, and a personal initiative, persistence, and commitment to students to make learning possible and meaningful. The balance of teacher-student control in the classroom may be a reflection of the teacher's level of trust in their students and the perceptions of their behaviors and underlying motivations.

Holding, healthy realistic expectations while encouraging students' input is essential in demonstrating the teacher's trust. Thus, when expectations don't exist and there is no structure in place, accompanied by low expectations, this is an extension of the everyday chaos students might be experiencing at home. No homework or class accountability goals "say that in life you will get a pass". We all know that students will not be exempt in life without being accountable.

As an educator, you have to ignore it when a child says, "I don't want to," or "I can't," because what they're saying is, "I don't think I can, and I need you to help me believe until I can believe."

Researchers found that schools suffer from the lack of trust by students and staff. Evidence of trust decreased for all students during middle school-sixth grade. Middle school is a critical time of development for all students. Middle school is when a student is most likely to first detect unjust policies or inequalities in the educational system. Due to the history of oppression in America, the decline of trust is much faster for Blacks, Latinos, and other minority students. Research further shows these students are more likely to be cited for behavior infractions the following year, even if they had never been in trouble before and received good grades. Public school records reveal that the racial disparity reported by many students did exist.

In each teaching situation, teachers may need to judge how much they trust their students in the different attributes of trust. For example, teachers may imagine their students to be honest, open, but not honestly well intentioned, but may not trust their students to be competent in their ability to handle a given academic assignment. A teacher who trusts her students to behave well, but does not believe they can do the academic work, may choose to modify her lesson plans. If the teacher, however, wishes to take her students on a field trip in which academic ability is not a requirement, she may feel she has a meaningful amount of trust in her students' honesty, openness, and benevolence to conduct the field trip.

For example, in the state of Missouri, 93 percent of teachers are white, 5 percent black, and 1.8 percent other races. Only 49 percent of teachers have only zero-to-ten years of experience, with a 6 percent decrease in the last ten years of trained teachers.

Research again supports the finding that white teachers, who comprise the vast majority of American educators, have far lower expectations for black students than they do for similarly situated white students.

EDUCATIONAL FACTS:

March 2014, the U.S. Department of Education Office for Civil Rights published data and statistics about school discipline

- ❖ 87 percent of all teachers in public schools are white.
- ❖ Black children represent 18 percent of preschool enrollment, but 48 percent receive more than one out-of-school suspension, while white students represent 43 percent of preschool enrollment and only 26 percent of out-of-school suspensions.

#1This evidence suggests that to raise student attainment and achievement, particularly among students of color, elevating teacher expectations, eliminating racial bias, and hiring a more diverse teaching force are worthy goals. So educational systems will need to recruit teachers straight out of college and co-op with area colleges and universities in the field of education.

When every student has the same value, it builds trust. Once a student trusts you, they will respect you. "We appreciate what we trust."

#2 Students cannot be devalued. You signed up to teach.

As educators, we are not reserved the right to teach only what we prefer. We cannot pull out what we prefer and put back what we dislike. Do we not have the option to put students back based on our preferences? We can't take the one we want, and throw back, and redraw again.

> ## Case Study
>
> Sixth grade student homeschooled since fifth grade, of Asian descent, with serious explosive and erratic behaviors. He struggles to adapt and understand socially, academically, and behaviorally in the general classroom setting. He lacks social skills to interact with peers. He has no individual educational plan nor has he been diagnosed by a trained mental health professional or Special Educational Services. The student reads on an eighth-grade level, but his writing is third-grade material.
>
> He has serious episodes of explosive anger, aggressiveness, and defiance where he throws objects in the classroom, elopes, walks out of class, threatens and curses out his teacher, roams the halls, climbs on and under the desk, crawls, and plays under tables. He is merely uncontrollable at times by his teachers and adminstrators. He can become out of control and shut down, falling out, yelling, and cursing. With these episodes, *is this student making the classroom an unsafe environment?*
>
> He responds to the cognitive-behavioral process because of the small environment and one-on-one, but he struggles in the general population. This works until he has to transition back to the classroom environment, where he is easily set off.
>
> Many of the student behaviors are associated with avoidance type behaviors. He also tends to get easily frustrated when he does not get the desired result (explosive tantrums). Student struggles to understand what is socially acceptable.

As a teacher: what is your first step in connecting and building trust with this student? How do you teach this student?

#3 As educators, we bring our environment into the classroom. They show up in writing referrals and dealing with our students.

Our brains are trained to categorize. Humans see skin color, gender, and age first because our brain responds to patterns; all humans use these associations to make judgments. It is not safe to say, "I don't see color or gender." It is precisely vital to see the two. That's culture. James Baldwin says it best "most humans live within a fantasy mind frame because of our emotional shallowness". No one wants to think they are biased, particularly not people who devote their time, money, and energy to a career of educating the next generation.

When bias affects the educator, he or she goes through at least five stages of distrust. The reasons are that the educator experiences expectations – broken promises, a pattern of unreliability.

1. Doubt
2. Suspicion
3. Anxiety-apprehension
4. Fear
5. Self-protection or withdrawal

DISCRIMINATION AGAINST BOYS IN THE CLASSROOM

Some boys can be a challenge for many educators because many of their problems deal with behaviors and moments of self-regulation and high levels of energy. For example, in implementing the emotional intelligence program for the Ritenour District's Middle School called **Discipline with Dignity** or **DWD,** data reveals black and brown boys were cited and sent to the Emotional Intelligence Room or DWD Room for more behaviors associated with fidgeting or expressing more motor activity such as horseplay, or expressing aggression in a joking matter.

According to Micheal Reichart and Richard Hawley, authors of **Reaching Boys, Teaching Boys**, boys are expelled from preschool almost five times more than girls, boys are more likely to drop out of school and less likely to do homework, and boys make up an increasingly low number of college graduates. The authors conclude that, since boys often receive lower grades than their test scores would predict, behavior-heavy grading practices penalize boys, particularly in the younger grades.[38]

Some research suggests boys' behaviors overshadow their academics. In Jawanza Kunjufu book, **Countering the Conspiracy to Destroy Black Boys**, he disagrees with that assumption. He believes that this is not accidental but intentional. Kunjufu ask the question of whether it's accidental that 35% of black and brown boys are have special education services and 50% of the black and brown boys incarcerated.[39] In my years of experience, many times, boys' behavior is misinterpreted based on color. In the state of Missouri, 93 percent of its teachers are white, while 5 percent are black and 1.8 percent are other races. While 78 percent of the teachers are females and only 21 percent are male, an alarming 49 percent of teachers have only zero-to-ten years of experience working with students. With an 83 percent minority student ratio, the teacher population does not reflect the same diversity as the student population. For minority boys, schools place discipline records and acting right in the classroom over academics. Black and brown boys are policed in the streets of Saint Louis heavily, and this is true in most urban cities as well as in the classroom. Minority boys are considered **intimidating bullies**, **aggressive**, **creators of unsafe environments**, **and disruptors of the class**. "Every time you do something, they are yelling, I am going to tell Dr. Dorsey, and I am writing you a referral." *8th-grade boy at HMS in St. Louis.*

Discipline Scenario

Sixth grade African American male, 5'9", weighs 246 pounds, with an Individual Education Plan.

Student's current data suggest nineteen documented teacher referrals with fifteen cited for **harassing** and **bullying behaviors** toward students. Student received another eight days for Out-School-Suspension (OSS).

Target Behaviors:
- Harassing, intimidating and bullying students and/or staff
- Fighting
- Creating an unsafe environment
- Disruptive school behaviors

Goals:
- Appropriate interaction with peers and adults
- Learn to use coping or calming strategies in times of frustration with a peer or adult

Strategies for improving target behaviors:
- Referral to C.H.A.D.S for counseling services
- Daily communication home to parent with return notifications
- Hallway Restriction – Student should not be released to take bathroom, drink, or locker breaks unless direct supervision is available. (Same is true when he is transitioning from one class to the next)
- Support from behavioral interventionists as needed.
- Daily check in with school counselor and social worker.

After student spent sevenconsecutives days in the DWD or EIL Learning Space, behaviors improved

---

Many difficult behaviors (e.g., off-task, out-of-seat, noisy) create constant demands for supervision or make the student stand out from others. Writing a referral or observation may provoke annoyance or be embarrassing. The information-gathering process need not be long or hard. It can be accomplished in the two steps below.

1. **Define challenging behavior.** The definition must be observable and highly descriptive of the behavior's appearance. "**Jesse is aggressive and runs from class,**" for example, is too vague and ambiguous. A better definition would be, "**Jesse will leave class or a designated activity area, often grabbing and damaging materials as he goes. If a staff person tries to keep him from leaving the area, he will strike out by grabbing, hitting, pulling hair, and/or kicking.**"

2. **Identify the circumstances under which the behavior is both likely and unlikely to occur.** The process of identifying these key circumstances may be either straightforward or involve varying amounts of detective work.[40]

DISCRIMINATION AGAINST GIRLS IN THE CLASSROOM

Teachers often reward girls for being quiet and having appropriate behavior rather than prompting them to seek more in-depth answers. Educational research and discipline data also reveals that teachers are more likely to interrupt girls openly during class discussions less likely to call girls to the front of the class, and less likely to direct their gaze toward girls while answering open-ended questions. As is true with most kinds of biases, teachers are often entirely unaware that they are treating their male and female students differently.

We all carry implicit bias, no matter where we come from. Implicit bias refers to unconscious attitudes, reactions, stereotypes, and categories that affect behavior and understanding.[41] In education, implicit bias often refers to unconscious racial or socioeconomic bias towards students, which can be as frequent as explicit bias. (Boysen)[42]

"Bias is woven through the culture like a silver cord woven through a cloth. In some situations, it's brightly visible. In others, it's hard to distinguish." (Jessica Nordell, *Is This How Discrimination Ends? Atlantic* (May 7, 2017).

Every teacher must be confident to take advantage of his or her discretionary space in the classroom. Discretionary space is the time allotted for the teacher to correct or address a situation. Discretionary time and space should be established at the beginning of the school year. The discipline must be consistent with the offense. Using the discretionary space, teachers make judgments in small moments.

1. Correcting off-task behaviors to increase focus. (There is a seven-second window)
2. Understanding your one-minute discretionary space for frequent judgment calls. This cannot wait.
3. Catching the smallest of the off-task behaviors and quickly refocusing the students is the best way to prevent more significant problems from occurring.
4. In dealing with the disruptive and disengaged students, teachers demonstrate their trust by encouraging them and by giving students second chances to behave appropriately.

Place an "X" in the box if the statement is true for you.
- ☐ I often wait too long before addressing a situation in the hope it will resolve itself.
- ☐ Because I do not want to hurt someone else's feelings or be the villain, I will tolerate unhealthy behavior.
- ☐ I sometimes use sarcasm around conflict, in hopes the student will get the point and I won't have to specifically address the situation.
- ☐ It is harder to address a conflict than it is to just put up with it
- ☐ I tend to address a conflict immediately without first thinking about the situation all the way through and allowing my emotions to subside.

REMEMBER

#1 ADJUST THE CLASSROOM ENVIRONMENT
- Whenever students are required to learn something new or to demonstrate what they know, there is an aspect of risk and push back The students must risk finding out that they are unable to learn the new skill, must risk looking dumb in front of others, and must risk getting a bad grade.

#2 ETHICAL CONSIDERATION: UNDERSTANDING BIAS
- No one wants to think they are biased, particularly not people who devote their time, money, and energy to teaching the next generation.
- Teacher's predispositions, beliefs, experiences, and abilities are likely to influence the level of trust.

#3 CONTINUUM OF CONSEQUENCES/ BEHAVIOR MANAGEMENT

- Catching the smallest of off-task behaviors and quickly refocusing the students is the best way to prevent more significant problems from occurring[43]
- In dealing with disruptive and disengaged students, teachers demonstrate their trust by encouraging them and by giving students second chances to behave appropriately

Below are classroom behaviors that are manageable by taking advantage of the discretionary space and opportunity.

- Out of seat
- Talking or making remarks during instructional time
- Inappropriate hallway behaviors
- Eating/drinking/chewing gum
- Inappropriate language
- Inappropriate technology use
- Horseplay
- Leaving without permission
- Throwing objects
- Sleeping in class
- Missing assignments
- Dress code violation
- Having no material
- Low level of vandalism

#4 SEVERAL ALTERNATIVE TEACHING STRATEGIES

- Shared Ownership: To create a classroom climate that is conducive to trust and promotes cooperation and learning, teachers require both skill (professionalism) and motivation. Group activities, real conversations, and shared ownership

#5 REINFORCED SUPPORTS FOR ADMINISTRATION

- Faculty links school trust with authenticity in school administrators' behavior and those actions of teachers and staff

SCHOOL HAS TO PROVIDE THREE TYPES OF DISCIPLINE:
PREVENTIVE, SUPPORTIVE, CORRECTIVE DISCIPLINE
PREVENTIVE : Persistence of ALL STAFF

FOCUS: A Thoughtful plan that incorporates everyone.
SUPPORTIVE: Effective Communication
CORRECTIVE: Firm but Fair

A Note to Educators:

- Good discipline is about understanding. Good discipline requires courage and creativity.
- Good discipline should focus on teaching, learning, and restorative processes after the punishment. Discipline is a part of every educator's job.
- Good discipline should trigger reflection and insight, the process of discussion, negotiation, and agreement or buy-in: the importance of discussion.
- Teachers should start fresh every day to keep optimism intact.
- Teachers should begin explaining the first day of school what kind of teacher you are and why. During the year, be willing to adapt your teaching style to different academic levels based on students.
- Ensure that your classroom rules are meaningful and significant
- Involve students to develop practical, appropriate consequences
- Treat students fairly by enforcing consistent rules while adapting individual results to fit circumstances.
- Traditional approaches, use of threats, punishment, rewards, are ineffective.
- Maintain a classroom that is structured, flexible and fair: this brings balance while meeting needs and maintaining social order.
- Remember, behavior change is slow and occurs in small increments.
- Collaborate with colleagues to foster a sense of community.
- We know every school has counselors, social workers, resources officers, and paraprofessionals, but teachers must listen to your students' thoughts and feelings.
- Use humor in your classroom.
- Understand that most middle school and upper grades students only have a maximum attention span of fifteen to twenty minutes, and younger children ten minutes.
- Offer choices with discipline and consequences.
- Good discipline requires short-term solutions without sacrificing long-term goals.
- Avoid shaming in the classroom; shaming consists of public embarrassment, and it will only worsen the behavior.

➢ Choices and limits go hand in hand when teaching responsibly. Too few restrictions can lead to rebellion or create narcissistic behavior; they have whatever they want.

➢ Be careful what you offer; don't take way privilege once it is provided. Do not include loss of opportunity as a threat.

Schools became a two-tiered system, with students who followed the rules rewarded and those who did not comply punished. What educators sometimes forget is that removing troublemakers from school does not eliminate them from life. Young adults who do not graduate from high school cost our society a fortune in expenses related to prison, welfare, and crime. Crime is one job that accepts anyone, regardless of educational status.

Today, we believe that rewards and punishments create winners and losers. This philosophy will not bring out the best in all students. We realized that many troubled students would not accept merely doing as they were told and would be more likely to comply if included in the decisions that affect their lives. We advocated for involving them in developing school and classroom rules and consequences, rather than imposing rewards.

Helpful Facts about Trust

The perception of trust in a classroom increases the willingness to risk this vulnerability in students and teachers (Tchannen-Moran & Hoy, 2000).

Teachers need to make realistic judgments about their students to maintain an appropriate amount of trust, a level of assurance that encourages students' growth and development while avoiding taking academic and social risks that are likely to result in diminishing the students' confidence, and a loss of learning opportunities.

Teachers and students may be impacted by prior experiences that may affect the level of trust they can develop. Teachers need to be aware that not all students begin school with the ability and skills necessary to meet the academic and behavioral expectations of their teacher. Besides, not all students have the knowledge or desire to participate in a positive, trusting relationship with their teacher.

Teachers who believe that their students can construct their learning may be more willing to engage in group activities, real conversations, shared ownership, and control of academic pursuits, with cultural differences as possible factors impacting teacher-student trust.

Students with disabilities are more than twice as likely to receive an out-of-school suspension at 13 percent versus students without disabilities at 6 percent.

Black students represent 16 percent of student enrollment but account for 27 percent referred to law enforcement and 31 percent subjected to a school-related arrest.

In ***Creative Strategies for Working with ODD (Oppositional Defiant Disorder) Children and Adolescents***, Frank, Paget, and Bowen suggest several "Houdini techniques" to escape from situations teachers may encounter with students with ODD.[44]

Some teachers' behaviors that unknowingly may add to power struggles in the classroom are:
- Threatening the student.
- Responding emotionally (i.e., getting angry or becoming sarcastic).
- Confronting the student openly or near their peers.
- Responding too quickly.
- Remaining in the interaction for too long.
- Using bribes.
- Trying to "convince."
- "Putting down" the student.

Diminishing Power Struggles: other strategies that may lessen power struggles include:
- Providing the student with simple directives and choices.
- Stating pre-determined consequences clearly before problems occur.
- Listening to the student before reacting.
- Giving brief and direct instructions in a calm tone.
- Discussing the issue privately with the student.
- Walking away before the situation gets too "hot."

The Power Struggle Reduction Plan: The authors also propose a power struggle reduction plan to prevent confrontations. These strategies include:
- Talk and work with another teacher. Agree to take over for each other.
- Pre-determine your consequences and then follow through.

- Decide which rules are negotiable and which are non-negotiable.
- When away from an incident, list all the things that hooked you into the power struggle.
- "Walk-by" reinforcements should be brief, even non-verbal, and minimal attention should be drawn.
- Whisper praises without bringing attention to the student. Leave a positive note for the student to discover.

The team approach used when developing an intervention plan to be implemented in the school, home, and community.

The team should be composed of teachers and other school professionals, but also psychologists, psychiatrists, and other medical professionals who work together to ensure the success of the student in a variety of settings. Listed below are strategies that have worked for us as parents, teachers, and team members. These strategies, when implemented consistently, have proven effective in teaching and parenting roles.

- Don't threaten unless you are willing to carry the threats out. Threatening students with ODD allows them to test your ability to follow through.
- Clearly define the behaviors you expect. Students with ODD often search for the "gray area" to justify their actions.
- Clearly define the consequences of compliant and non-compliant behavior. This provides a direct relationship between the desired or undesired behavior and the respective result and prevents "fueling" an argument.
- Always be firm and consistent. Students with behavioral issues are continually looking for an "open gate" and an opportunity to challenge your directives or justify their position. [45]
- During confrontations, do not allow your emotions to rule. With students with ODD, your anger demonstrates that they are in control. Behave like Clint Eastwood in *Dirty Harry* — stay cool, calm, and collected under the most challenging situation.

Although students can challenge teachers and parents, they can be our leaders tomorrow. If directed positively, they can take control of a situation and make things happen. By building on the students' strengths and allowing them to achieve success, students with ODD will feel good about their capabilities and become productive members of society.

TRUST ACTIVITIES FOR A RESTORATIVE CIRCLE

1. Why is **TRUST** important in building relationships?
2. Why do you struggle with **trusting most adults**? Tell me about a time when an adult let you down.
3. How do you deal with your **anger** when your **trust** has been violated?
4. What are some healthy steps to gain **trust**?
5. Why is **trust** important in friendship?
6. What is positive communication?
7. How can you handle your emotions when you are upset?

CLASSROOM LESSONS: CAN BE CREATED IN A MICROSOFT POWERPOINT

1. What part of the brain produces anger?
2. What is the actual definition of anger?
3. Where does anger come from in the brain? What part of the brain is responsible for anger?
4. What are some physiological signs of anger?
5. What are your first signs of anger?
6. What is the survival brain?
7. What can you do to manage your anger?

Sometimes trauma imprints itself beyond what language can reach.

Music can change your brain: the rhythm and tone become synched with the heart, and music can alter students' lives. It can affect the way of thinking, your mood, while stimulating your feeling (both positive or negative and even compulsion).46

Chapter Six

MUSIC AND SOCIAL-EMOTIONAL DEVELOPMENT

Music holds a crucial role in our society,[47] and the creation and consumption of music represent a universal human activity.[48]

Did you know that exposure to music can improve learning and increase positive classroom atmosphere? (Eerola & Eerola, 2013; Foran, 2009)[49]

There is a long and rich tradition of using music to cultivate resilience and facilitate healing in the wake of violence and oppression. Songs and chanted hymns often accompanied physical labor endured by American slaves to coordinate movement and boost resolve to complete arduous tasks.[50]

Students come to my band classes, as they do all their classes, in various moods: mostly happy, but sometimes angry or sad or depressed about something going on with them or with a friend or family member.

Band is a class they enjoy, so most of the time, sometimes not, if a student is angry or down about something, and I see that, I will talk to them in my office about what is going on and give them the option of just following along that day with their music in the folder but not rehearsing with the rest of the class. Students will choose to go ahead and rehearse because playing their instrument with the class usually puts them in a better mood and at least temporarily it takes their mind off their issues or situation. It is very refreshing to see students come to class not happy, but leave the class with a smile on their face, because they chose to participate in the band rehearsal.

Mr. McDaniel-Saint Louis County Public School

Music in the classroom has BENEFITS

- Reduces feelings of anxiety and stress.
- Helps children regulate their emotions
- Music, memory, and emotions are linked. This initial study found that "music serves as a potent trigger for retrieving memories"
- Improves concentration and on-task behaviors
- Enhances the way children can process language and speech

Music registers with the dopamine chemical, the motivation chemical in our brains, which is responsible for preservation and rewards.

Emotional responses to music are neurally mediated, such that listening to music activates brain structures involved in reward, pleasure, and emotional processing (e.g., insula, ventral medial prefrontal cortex, ventral striatum, amygdala, hippocampus; Koelsch 2009).[51]

MUSIC CALMS AGGRESSIVE BEHAVIOR

Several studies on the effects of experiencing calm music have suggested that it can reduce aggressive behavior and regulate moods, particularly feelings of anxiety and stress.[52]

Exposure to neighborhood violence has a much more significant impact than we think it does," said the lead author, Johns Hopkins sociologist Julia Burdick-Will, an assistant professor at the Johns Hopkins School of Education. "It seeps into places that you don't expect. It can affect an entire school and how it's able to function."

Accordingly, negative feelings such as anger, guilt, shame, fear, and anxiety may be addressed by music's ability to activate reward pathways in the brain and suppress the release of stress hormones (Chanda & Levitin, 2013; Cepeda, 2006, Thayer & Levenson, 1983). Music may also help those with anhedonia or muted emotional experiences, as it can access neural pathways to emotion previously down-regulated in response to the index trauma (DeNora, 2002; Saarikallio & Erkkila, 2007).

LISTENING TO MUSIC ENHANCES INTELLIGENCE

Listening to music could enhance intelligence; some studies have been widely refuted.[53] The University of Maryland Medical Center reveals that students should listen to music and it is proven to help reduce stress! Music is an effective stress reducer in both healthy individuals and people with health problems. There are still many benefits of listening to music while studying. Background music may improve focus on a task by providing motivation and improving mood.

Anxiety stricken students should listen to music using ear buds before heading into a room for example a library. This helps them deal with isolation and structure of quietness. They will feel relaxed, at ease, and ready to conquer chapter after chapter. The University of Maryland School of Music and Medical Center suggest that listening to soothing music can decrease blood pressure, heart rate, and anxiety levels in heart patients".[54]

MUSIC HELPS STUDENTS FOCUS MORE

Music rewires the brain through harmonization to show attentiveness to specific attention. Music helps the brain to pay attention to detail. Researchers utilizing musical compositions from the 1800s found that "music engages the areas of the brain involved with paying attention, making predictions, and updating the event in memory" (Baker). They believed that music choice was influential on brain processing.[55]

IMPROVE PERFORMANCE

Scientifically music helps structure the brain through rhythmic tones, thus releasing endorphins and thus slowing the reaction to high-pressure situations. Music is processed on the right side of the brain, creating an access point to the limbic system. It has the power to create calmness. *USA Today* asks, "Want to sink the game-winning shot when the pressure is on? Basketball players listen to some upbeat tunes before the big game." [56]

PROVEN TO IMPROVE BRAIN FUNCTIONS

Children who interact with music at early and earlier stages in life have improved cognitive performance. Music helps your brain function! Background music may enhance performance on cognitive tasks. Music is the key to math that elevates thinking and improves the overall purpose of the brain. Listening to music allowed test takers to complete more questions in the time allotted and get more answers right.

The American Psychological Association, in 2013, defined resilience as "the process of adapting well in the face of adversity, trauma, tragedy, threats, or significant sources of threat." Music therapy is considered a resilience-enhancing intervention as it can help trauma-exposed individuals harness their ability to recover elements of normality in their life following great adversity.

Chapter Seven

BRINGING HEALING BACK INTO THE CLASSROOM WITH CIRCLES

"Let the circle be unbroken."

The formation of a **circle** conveys a sense of community in the classroom. The circle statement, as used in many ancient tribal cultures such as African and native/indigenous people, speaks communication, and this a safe space to talk and become united. The circle's purpose is to bring restoration and seeks to develop healthy relationships while connecting the community. Across the fifty-four African countries, circles were the most potent expression of the African people. "Let the circle be unbroken" is a popular conviction throughout Africa. Circles represent interrelated skills sets of a common purpose like your keys of music in the last chapter they correlate in sequence and connect with the same motive of a beginning, and close. Circles give each child the avenue to be unique and have a purpose but also belong to the community and contribute to its mission. This philosophy goes against the Western culture of individualism and self-grandeur.

The First Nation "Aboriginal" used circles in a restorative form called restorative circles as generally healing circles. The restorative circles repaired the harmful and the injured, any results of an offense, including the offender, elder, and victim. Healing circles were called "hocokah," meaning sacred circle. These circles included talking circles, praying circles, and being committed to helping one another toward healing.[57]

Educators can use healing circles for various reasons. Whether for reason or practice, restorative practices are about changing attitudes and connecting. Circles can set ground rules for a new project or activity or deal with a severe personal injury in the class.

Below are ways a classroom can use circles:
1. **Student Check-ins:** At the beginning of the class and /or academic semester students can discuss performance goals or behavioral goals within the circle. **Example:** What is one of your class performance goals or academic goals today-this year? Name (1) outcome-based behavioral goal today?
2. **Student Check-out:** What is one thing you have learned today?
3. **Classroom Norms and Expectation:** In our class community we value... (please complete the statement)
4. **Content and Assignments**
5. **Behavior Problems:** We have experienced some non-community-like behavior in our class space. It is visible and hurtful. We can improve this safe space of community by demonstrating what types of behaviors.
6. **Establishing Community**
7. **Addressing Inequities – Promoting Unity**

Expect Resistance and Resentment

Having courageous conversations and building community in the classroom may seem difficult. Jane Elliot, on April 5, 1968, set out to start a needed conversation when she took her third-grade class in rural Iowa through a race experiment, which is nationally known as the Blue Eye Brown Eye Activity. Throughout this activity, students gathered in circle formation to discuss the effects of segregation and color discrimination. Jane Elliot taught twenty-eight students not to be prejudiced, but to see each person based on content and character. As with any courageous conversation, there will be reluctance.

Conversations and opportunities to grow a child from self-reliance to opening up and communicating, there will be a reluctance to do so. Students may be reluctant in the beginning to participate after introducing the circles practices. As a facilitator, this view is only fear-based reluctance; often, students have been trained by their environment not to share openly or to express their thoughts in a public setting. By becoming proactive at the onset, you can use a variety of talking tools to assist as a conversation starter. Make sure the objects do not distract from the process. Please do not use bouncy objects such as balls. Students will help each other during the process. This becomes a circle of empowerment.

Educators, make sure to,
- Set precise topic and goal for the outcomes; please prepare, not off the cuff
- Stay positive, proactive, focused
- Sit in the circle with the students
- Be creative
- Be prepared for pleasant and unpleasant feelings

Circles can be a very healthy practice for middle school through high school students when conflict has caused a disruption. Teachers can begin by asking questions using the circle method. In conducting this restorative practice, praise students openly to allow students to regain a good name. Make sure all parties are willing and invested in the process.

- What was your part in the problem or conflict?
- What part did you add to the conflict?
- How can we make sure this does not happen again?
- How do you feel when the same behaviors were directed toward you?

Note to the Teachers:
I know you may feel unprepared for this or feel you do not have time for it, but you do. note to the teacher. No, you're not a counselor or social worker, but in some instances, you are by interacting with the child you can help them relate and also increase your productivity. You are with these students at least 188 calendars day out of 365 days of a year for at least seven hours a day.

Two important truths about education
#1: Most educators are uncomfortable approaching challenging students; they feel discipline is not their job.
#2: Administrators are too burdened to deal with individual class management issues, which puts the school at enormous risk.

Healing and Community Circle Format

Everyone can share valuable insight.

Circle

Keeper/Centering Moment

Begin with a deepbreathing exercise

(Breathe. Take a breath)

or a 2 min.**Mindfulness Exercise**

Every student pick from the affirmation cards to share.

Circle Keeper creates affirmation cards using colorful index cards.

Circle Keeper introduces the "Talking Piece"

Circle Keeper: Shares the purpose of the circle is to strengthen and deepen respect for the classroom connection and build community.

You are encouraged to share and please feel free to pass if unable to share.

Circle Keeper: Today we want to understand each other better.

Can you tell us how you feel?

Today I am... Mad, Happy, Grateful, Sad, etc.

I feel happy when:

I feel mad when:

I feel excited when:

Etc.

How can you feel safe in this classroom or school?

What do you need right now so we can meet your need?

Round 2

Name the person you would like to share your Excitement with...

Circle Keeper: Close and Share a Positive Quote

STUDENT PEACEFUL RESOLUTION AGREEMENT

Student One and ***Student Two*** agree that we have had a continual conflict. This conflict has strained our relationship and added problems to our friends and shared space. We have chosen not to work towards mending this relationship. On ***date*** in our peaceful resolution session, we agree that

1. We will not speak on or regarding each other. We will not have further contact with one another: verbal, physical, social-media, or invite ourselves into the other's friendship space.
2. We will not agitate the situation by discussing it further with friends or associates.
3. We will do disrupt the learning environment by bringing this drama to our classroom space.
4. We accept that we are unable to be friends nor do we desire friendship
5. We will remain at a healthy physical distance without conflict.
6. If a situation should occur, we will speak to our grade-level counselor or trusted adult to assist us with our perceptions.

We agree that we can share the **(School)** space without further conflicts such as arguments and fighting.

(Student1)_____   Date_____

(Student2)_____   Date_____

Instructor_____

Restorative Classroom Agreement

We agree that the classroom is the place of shared cooperative learning.

Teacher's name and **the student name** have entered into a (TS) Teacher–Student mutual agreement of trust and learning on **date,** at _____ Middle School.

Restorative Steps

1. _____ agrees to share with _____ the status of her day. There may be times the student may not be in the best emotional space.

2. In the case of class disruptions, both agree that two firm redirections should be given to address any form of disruptive behavior.

3. _____ agrees to call home to give parents an update after the redirections are given.

_____ agrees to participate as a cooperative student, assisting others with help if needed, and getting all of her classroom work completed.

_____ agrees to gentle and firm redirections, providing one (10-minute) break in Social Studies or Math as needed, and an assigned seat to help with focusing and staying on task.

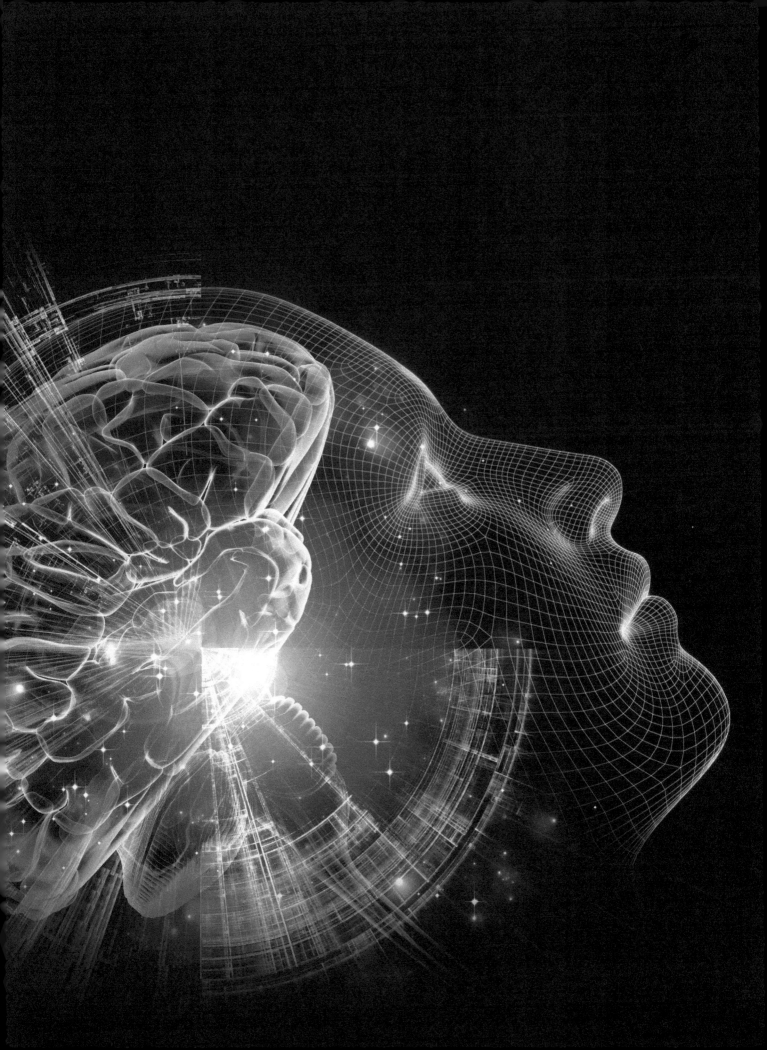

Part Two

The Comprehensive guide to implementing an Emotional Intelligence Learning Program

Helping students navigate through negative emotional behaviors to respond and cope in more positive manners.

Reflective Engagement

Cognitive Engagement

Behavioral Engagement

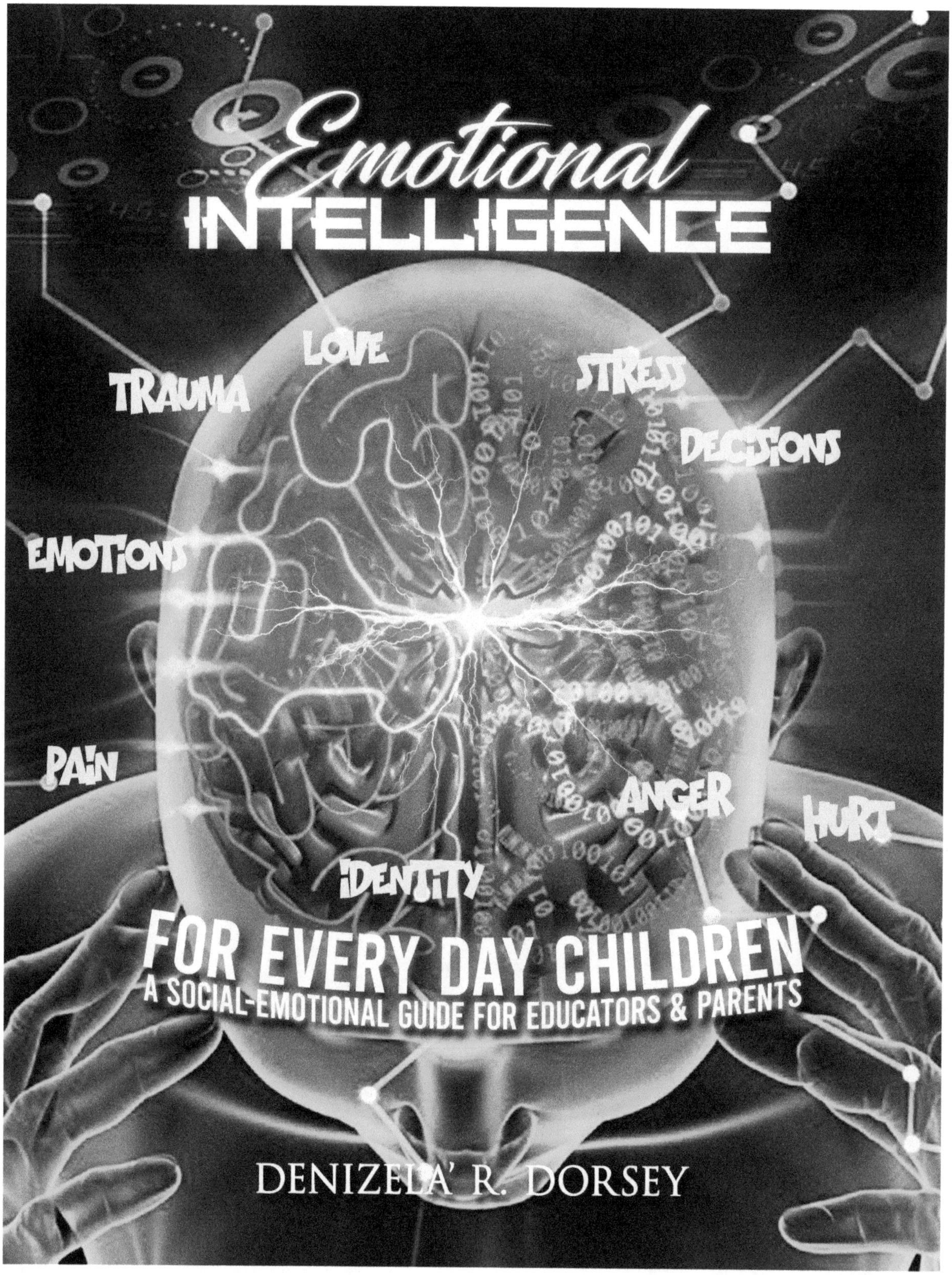
Emotional
INTELLIGENCE
LOVE
TRAUMA
STRESS
DECISIONS
EMOTIONS
PAIN
ANGER
HURT
IDENTITY
FOR EVERY DAY CHILDREN
A SOCIAL-EMOTIONAL GUIDE FOR EDUCATORS & PARENTS
DENIZELA' R. DORSEY

COMPREHENSIVE APPROACH TO EMOTIONAL INTELLIGENCE

Helping students navigate through negative emotional behaviors to respond and cope in more positive manners.

(Notes and Thoughts)

PREFACE:

This method is rooted in academic excellence, personal enrichment activities, and restorative practices to support all students toward healthy behavioral intervention and target the inappropriate behaviors. By implementing each lesson participants expand their spheres of moral reasoning and improve their critical thinking skills. Each lesson can be adapted to meet your educational need.

We must remember that intelligence is not enough. Intelligence plus character—that is the goal of true education. –Dr. Martin Luther King Jr.

The goal is to build **C.H.A.R.A.C.T.E.R**
Self-**Awareness**
Self-**Regulation**
Self-**Motivation**
Social **Skills**

EDUCATING STUDENT WITH **A.R.M.S.**

Four Essential Functions for "Everyday Students" as Emotional Intelligent Learners:

- ❖ <u>**Social Competence**</u>: Classroom and Social Engagements: School Classroom Managed Behaviors: Preparedness, Understanding and Accepting Classroom Expectations and Instructions
- ❖ <u>**Social Interactions**</u>: Interactions within the peer and school environment without aggressive language, threats, harassments of students or teachers, or foul language.
- ❖ <u>**Self-Management and Self-Regulation**</u>: Thinking, Feeling, Doing: Behavior Reflections and Think Sheets
- ❖ <u>**Self-Awareness and Cognition**</u>: Emotional Stability, Positive Boundaries, Healthy Verbal and Nonverbal Communication
  - ➤ **Personal Boundaries**: limits that are set in place for personal safety, healthy, emotionally well

> ➤ **Emotional Boundaries**: Developing healthy emotional responses
> ➤ **Physical Boundaries**: Understanding and respecting personal space and standards

OVERVIEW/WHY/PURPOSE/AUDIENCE

Aspects of Emotionally Intelligent Learning Program (EIP)

Academic Preparedness and Readiness (Success that builds for the future)

Social Skills (inside and outside classroom and school environment)

Character Education

Individual Planning

Behavior Intervention Support

Developing EIP Strategy Teams with your Building

Building Principal or Assistant Principal

Grade Level School Counselors

School Social Worker

Behavioral Supports and Interventionist

School Mentor or Check-In Staff

Special School District Staff or Individual Education Team

Educational Team (English Language Art, Math, Science, Social Studies, Reading and Math Specialist Teachers and Professional)

Next Steps: Define or create the Layout of **EIP Classroom Structure**. Entry points for all students? Why will a student spend time in the **EIP** Classroom?

WHY

Why does every school need Emotionally Intelligent learning spaces or a CHILL Space?

Why is it important in an educational setting?

1. Emotionally Intelligence School-Based Program addresses:

Positive behavior supports and social-emotional learning program: EIP is not an in-school suspension or policing program or a storehouse for "bad kids."

Emotionally Intelligence Program offers evidence-based practices

- **Education about Teenage Brain Theory * Emotions * Trauma * ACES (Adverse Childhood Experiences Survey)**

- **Restorative Justice Processes in the School or Classroom**
- **Conflict and Peace Resolution and Mediation**
- **Anger Management and De-escalation Methods**
- **(Advocacy) and Equity: Voices for Students and Teachers**
- **Safe Space for CHILL, RESET, and REFOCUS**
  Academic Support helping struggling students get caught up on academics

2. **Things you should know and understand in the EIP positions: EIP Instructor and Social-Emotional Family Support.**
   - How to build positive relationships and the importance of building positive relationships
   - How to advocate for students and teachers
   - The importance of trust and confidentiality with students and teacher-staff
   - Understanding mental illness and how to identify mental illness in the educational setting **(ADHD/ADD, OHI, ODD, Emotional Disturb, Anxiety, Self-Injury-Cutting, Depression, Eating Disorders, Social Media, Substance Abuse: Marijuana Usage, Vaping)**
   - How to identify when students are having an emotional breakdown
   - The difference between spectrum outburst vs learned behavior tantrum (SSD understanding)
     Brian Science/Triune Brain: Frontal Lobe/Limbic System/Brain Stem (Reptilian Brain)
   - Self-regulation vs dysregulation
   - Task Avoidance
   - What are defiance and defiance-associated behaviors?
   - What is a social and emotional interventionist role (How both work together)
     - Tiers Behaviors (I, II, III)
     - The effects of trauma bonding
     - Understanding Systematic Racism and Bias
     - Global Assessment Functioning Scale
     - How environment can influence educational setting
     - Understand Cultural Stereotypes
     - Knowledge in working with diverse populations
     - Understand Language barriers to education
     - Understand the Theory of White Privilege

WHO
3. Who will you work with: We are a part of a universal social and emotional team.
Teachers: Other Staff
Administration, Counselors, Social Workers
Special School District Staff
Entire School

WHEN
Meetings to attend in the building. New School Year Transitional Planning, Meetings to discuss students with social and emotional needs to setup Supports. Building meetings with Counselors, Administrators, Special School District Teachers and Staff, and attend all school-wide professional development seminars.

4. **Data Collecting**
   1. **Average Number of Students seen**
      A. Social-Emotional Supports
      B. Reset-Refocus Students
      C. Chill passes used during the day

5. **What are the infractions?**
Physical altercation or fighting, aggressive outburst, eloping, physical destruction of property, disrespect, defiance, extreme aggressive horseplay, paraphernalia, verbal altercation or verbal assault, after-school missed detention, conflict with teachers or peers mediation (home-related trauma), vandalism, classroom disruptions, talking back, task-avoidance, others.

6. **What is the student population and grade level with the highest behavior concerns?**
EIP data supports in elementary third and fourth-graders may demonstrate more social emotional needs.
Elementary School: Third and Fifth graders with trauma higher referrals
Middle School: Sixth and Seventh –graders...
High School: Ninth and Tenth-graders
   • Include the ratio between boys and girls

What findings does your data support? Examples are below of a Saint Louis County Public School.

1. Current school environment is distrustful (trust level is broken in classroom and within building among students, teachers, and staff).
2. Disparity of race representation in classroom and among teaching staff. Non-minority teachers struggle to understand cultural difference with their students.
3. Healthy classroom management skills vs unhealthy management skills.
    A. Teachers who are not trained in behavioral management.
    B. Teachers struggle to identify unhealthy behaviors.
4. Gaps in communication and ways to close them. No cohesiveness as a building.
5. Non-existing structure in the classroom
6. Grouping too many high needs behaviors in the same classroom.
7. Not enough efforts made to build positive relationships.

School Blind Spots
1. Be aware of the bias you haven't acknowledged. (Be sure not pass judgment, based on biases according to actions)
    *   When students are sent to the office, a majority of the time it is students of color (i.e., AA or His.) or suspicion based on what was told by other students of other races.
    *   Easier for students of color to be sent out due to the fact of preferential treatment based on biases.
2. Stepping out of our mental model of what students are capable of…. "students of color are not good at math, science and physical education are much easier for them."
3. Work hard to see students as capable individuals regardless of race or physical appearance/gender.

Power Struggles: Successful Techniques for Teachers:
1. In class relationship building, create an activity that helps support students becoming engaged/accountable

2. Prevention Strategies: Create opportunities for students to take an active role in the classroom by being in charge of something or taking an active leadership role
3. Intervention Strategies: Stay connected to students without taking what they say and do personally. AQTIP **(Adults Quit Taking It Personally)** Reframing situations, helping students see things from another student's perspective
4. De-escalation Strategies: Diffusing situation quickly, timing is very important
5. Power Struggle Scenario: What do you do when a student runs in a hallway
6. Seating students properly in class
7. Have students decode messages other students say
8. Communicating about major crisis, using reframing techniques

RECOMMENDATIONS FOR A SCHOOL DISTRICT TO PROMOTE EMOTIONAL INTELLIGENCE

P roven practices that can transform a school district's climate, promoting healthy social-emotional practices and trauma-informed systems. These practices are taught to leaders and implemented across America in rural and urban Public Schools: Kansas, Missouri, Georgia, Ohio, and North Carolina. These practices create a trauma-sensitive environment with Emotional Intelligence.

Creating a trauma-sensitive environment with emotional intelligence will require the following:

REMEMBER: An organization is only as strong and competent as its leaders. Healthy leaders produce healthy organizations.

1. Starting emotional intelligence trauma sensitivity at the early childhood development stages: Kindergarten. Requires K-12 learning opportunities for staff and parents.
2. Adopting a strength perspective model for the entire district, teaching emotional intelligence and trauma district-wide. The strength perspective originated from the University of Kansas. It focuses on strength-based practices with solution focus modeling producing long-term success rate.
3. Providing family and parental supports for the working class and transient communities. Enrichment seminars for the parents that focus on resources such as mental health evaluations, health assessment, healthy nutrition, and best practices. Providing recourses to migrant families. Providing small incentives for families to attend meals, gas vouchers, etc. Accessing needs of the learning community with a strength-based focus

4. Launch wraparound health services in the district, a center where families can access health care. Mental health services and screening

5. Developing hiring practices that reflect the core values of the school district: 1. Creating a culture of excellence on every grade level. When organizations set expectations, people will rise to the occasion. 2. Providing relevant professional training for staff (equity & cultural competency, test-taking strategies, soft skills, debating for students, revising math & science curriculum, and reading and language as core) 3. Keeping cultural competency training at the forefront and ongoing. 4. Equipping staff and teachers with classroom management skills on how to handle students with traumatic pasts. 5. Developing a district discipline policy using a restorative justice model on every grade level. 6. Encompassing character education on every grade level. 7. Hiring a competent professional who loves their jobs Providing alternative learning for those students who struggle in an in-class setting

6. Using vision boards for all grade levels

7. Improving teacher-student relationships

8. Teachers and administrators who understand their roles in the impact on students' lives

9. Build positive relationships with parents

10. Incorporate interdisciplinary teams at every grade level to support students

Program Components

Component #1:

EXAMPLE: EIP Social-Emotional Middle School Classroom Structure

☐ Pick Students up from Student Reporting Area

☐ Breakfast 7:45-8:00

Entering classroom, students complete *Entrance Reflections Sheet*

☐ **Classroom Expectations and Guidelines**:(*Instructor will cover ten minutes*)

☐ **This is a safe interactive and reflective classroom. Cellphones are not permitted, cellphones distract from class purposes. Please turn in your cellphone and receive it back at the end of the day.**

☐ **For safety, students you are to remain seated in your assigned seat at all times.**

☐ You are encouraged to participate in class activities and discussions. Please agree to keep the confidence of your peers and any personal information shared while participating in-group.

☐ Students, you may check out calming tools or sit in a fidget seat to assist in self-regulation.

☐ Please follow the school technology guidelines. We do not use school technology for personal use of SnapChat, FB, Instagram, Twitter, etc.

☐ In this interactive and reflective classroom, students, you are not to talk without permission. Students, you will be asked to participate in group discussions.

☐ Students, you are expected to complete all grade level assignments today. No work will be taken home. All schoolwork assigned is due the next school day.

☐ Sleeping and laying your head down on your desk will not be allowed. Students should remain awake, alert, and engaged.

☐ You will be given at least three positive verbal warnings and/or a redirection, and a conversation before consequences.

☐ Students will be asked to read and work to complete a narrative reflective essay of three to seven pages.

☐ Students, you are not allowed to leave the room except at your designated times. Bathroom breaks, lunch, and exiting. All walkouts will result in administrative consequences.

Component #2:

Example of a Social Emotional Schedule for EIP Middle School Classroom

☐ **Morning Restroom Break:**   9:30 AM & 1 PM

☐ **Lunch**   10:38 AM

   Students pick up trays in Cafe—Take trays to classroom to eat.

☐ **Presentations and Evaluations**   1:30

☐ **Dismissal**   2:15 PM   Done

☐ GOALS

1. Accept responsibility for your actions
2. Create a next step behavioral plan for ourselves
3. Respond appropriately to the instructions

4. Complete all assignments: Grade level assignments for subject area: Math, ELA, Social Studies, Science and reflections sheet

☐ *Character Lesson* responsive to student needs: thirty minutes
Character Videos
Group Discussion
  ☐ *Reading* and *Literacy Component* (working in collaboration with school's librarian and reading specialist
  ☐ **Group Restroom Break**
  ☐ **Individual Grade Level Assignment**
  ☐ **One-on-One Individual Talk Time**
  ☐ **Lunch in the Classroom**

Noon: *Character Lesson* responsive to student needs: thirty minutes
Character Videos
Group Discussion
  ☐ **Break Time/ TA:** Subject to change at the discretion of instructor

  ☐ **Individual Grade Level Assignment Work Time**

  ☐ **Exiting Reflection Sheets (*Nextstep Self-Assessment*)**

  ☐ **2:30 Exit and Dismal**

Upon dismissal from Classroom: Conferencing with counselors and teacher

Visits:
  A. Parent will be informed of first visit to EI Classroom.
  B. After five visits to the EI Classrooms; parents will be called by school counselors to schedule a (Moving Forward) Restorative Justice Plan using Student Profile 2000.
  C. Restorative Justice Reflection Sheet will be completed by student.

Component #3:
OUTCOMES YOU WILL EXPERIENCE WITH THE EIL SOCIAL-EMOTIONAL CLASSROOM

CELEBRATIONS:
- Program works (proven effectiveness)
- Students appreciate the calm learning environment
- Students like individual assistance with academics
- Reduction of OSS increasing
- Mediation process proven effective
- Teachers have positive communication with their EIP Instructor
- Students are very knowledgeable about teenage brain development and self-regulations
- Reduction in recidivism of previous year's frequent flyers
- Positive performance in academic achievement

I. STRESS ASSOCIATED WITH EIP ENVIRONMENT
A. Reinforce classroom maximum number of ten students. When the **EIP** classroom is ten students or more it becomes less therapeutic, focusing on controlling behaviors or a containment classroom.

B. Understanding and revisiting the behavior chart for students assigned to the Social-Emotional Classroom (Decision-Making Flow Chart)
1. Fighting intervention
2. Bullying
3. Peer relationships
4. Defiance
5. Inappropriate language
6. Establishing a teacher-student relationship
7. Dysregulated students
8. Safe place for teachers
9. ALT EDU setting
10. Academic safe place

C. It's important to set aside one day out of the month to track social-emotional data to review effectiveness.

D. Continue to improve communication with admin of why students are placed in social-emotional classroom.

E. Social-emotional instructors need to be actively involved in the behavioral planning process of students.

EIP SOCIAL-EMOTIONAL JOB DESCRIPTION:

A social-emotional behavior specialist is a professional with master's-level professional training in social work, psychology, social sciences, or licensed master's-level educator with experience in trauma-informed practices working with diverse populations.

Implements scientifically supported educational, behavioral, and mental health interventions consistent with trauma-informed universals (regulation, mindfulness strategies, parts of brain, sensory activities, and understands windows of stress tolerance).

Focuses on helping students with social and emotional needs achieve their potential in the classroom.

- ☐ Conducting small groups
- ☐ Serving as a resource to school staff members in the development of a balanced program for social/emotional needs of students
- ☐ Supporting teachers in observing, describing, proactively teaching and responding to social/emotional needs
- ☐ Participating in Individual Educational Plan meetings
- ☐ Collaborate with classroom teachers and other school staff members
- ☐ Implement strategies for the student's daily activities.
- ☐ Provide information and support to parents and families when appropriate.
- ☐ Provide professional development on topics concerning students with behavior needs.

See more interventions in the back of the book

C — Challenge yourself to excel beyond expectations

H — Help others to see the greatness in you by seeing the greatness in yourself

A — Apply a positive attitude

R — Respect yourself and those around you

A — Accept challenges as opportunity for growth

C — Choose wisely even when your decision is not popular

T — Trust that your hard work, dedication, and readiness will payoff

E — Excellence in Performance and Expectations

R — Rise above all obstacles and circumstances and moving beyond them

CHILL PASS: PERMISSION TO REPLICATE

PLEASE EXCUSE ME. I NEED A FEW MINUTES TO TAKE A BREAK TO CALM DOWN

C ALM DOWN

H ANG A BIT

I NEED A FEW MINUTES

L IKELY NOT THE SITUATION

L EARNING TO GET BETTER

CHILL PASS

GRANTED PERMISSION TO COPY

Activity/ Lessons

Creating Character scenarios: thinking beyond
the superficial? What does life look like and
what does life mean as a young person?

AWKWARDNESS

REBELLION CENTER

LOVE

EGO

PERSONALITY FLUCTUATION

LOVE FOR THE PARENT / CAREGIVER

HATE FOR THE PARENT / CAREGIVER

READING-WRITING-SOLVING MATH

SELF IMAGE

ADDICTION TO SOCIAL MEDIA + CELL PHONE

Emotional INTELLIGENCE

Lesson: (C)

CHALLENGING YOURSELF

Quotes about challenging yourself.

If it does not challenge you, it does not change you. Name One (Thing) in your behavior that needs challenging, according to you? And Why?

Challenge yourself every day to do better and be better. Growth starts with one small decision. Name one small decision that you are going to make.

Constantly challenge yourself every day.

The worst mistake you can make when you're young is to give up on yourself. Name one thing that you are not going to give up on.

Challenge yourself to overcome fear or failure. Name one fear.

This is your time (today), your moment, so make the most of it. Be awesome and push yourself. Name one thing that makes you awesome.

If you never challenge yourself, you will never know your potential.
1. What does **challenging yourself** mean to you?
2. What does **challenging yourself** look like?
3. What is the feeling of **challenging yourself**?
4. Who are people you know who have **challenged themselves**?
5. What are your **steps** in **challenging yourself?**

WORKSHEET: WHO ARE YOU?

I would like to introduce:

- <u>Who am I</u>

Words that can describe your personality:

Deep Thinker	Leader	Trustworthy	Happy
Hard Worker	Loud and disrespectful	Followers	I am a good kid
Adventurous	Popular	Argumentative	I am a thief
Show-off	Stubborn	Con	Adaptable
Responsible	Unpopular	Sad	Competitive

Name some of the schools you have attended.

Your family consists of

Things that your family cares about?

School behaviors that your family doesn't like or deems unacceptable.

Future ambitions?

One thing you do well?

In the space below write your name by creating words from the letters in your name to describe you.

_____

_____

_____

_____

_____

_____

_____

_____

_____

_____

_____

_____

_____

_____

_____

Lesson:

HELP OTHERS:

Seeing Greatness in Yourself

"I have personal pride in self, schoolwork, and behavior."
Speak positively over yourself.
"I can encourage myself."

Quotes for Personal Pride

By building healthy relationships we create a source of love and personal pride and belonging that makes living in a chaotic world easier.

Pride is a personal commitment. It is an attitude which separates excellence from mediocrity.

—William Blake

Disciplining yourself to do what you know is right and important, although difficult, is the highroad to pride, self-esteem, and personal satisfaction.

— Margaret Thatcher

We learn early on that, in order to be a winner, you have to believe in yourself. You have to have the confidence to make things happen. And you have to have personal pride.

— Alan Cohen

My life has a mission.

      I am here to do...

Taking care of myself.

      I take care myself by...

I can learn from my mistakes?

Quotes about learning from mistakes.

"We are products of our past, but we don't have to be prisoners of it."
— Rick Warren

"Many times what we perceive as an error or failure is actually a gift. And eventually we find that lessons learned from that discouraging experience prove to be of great worth."

— Richelle E. Goodrich

Name one mistake you have made in school. What did you learn from the mistake?

Don't get in your own way!

Five Star Tips for holding your**self accountable**.

1. Own it
2. Monitor yourself; know your triggers.
3. Set goals for yourself
4. Learn coping strategies for not getting what you want.
5. Ask for what you need, and ask for help.

I have the tools to create my future.

My tools are?

MY ACCOUNTABILTY TOOL BOX

Lesson: (A)
APPLY A POSITIVE ATTITUDE.

Winning Attitude:

I CAN DO IT
SLOW DOWN THE SPEED OF YOUR EMOTIONS
MAKE SURE YOU CAN COMMIT
MAKE NO EXCUSES
AVOID THE WRONG PEOPLE

Winning at Life

SURROUND YOUR SELF WITH THOSE WHO WILL AND CAN HELP YOU
PRACTICE YOUR GIFT
SET 1 PERSONAL GOAL

Man in the Mirror Exercise

BE TRUE TO YOURSELF
THERE IS ONLY ONE YOU, SO BE THE BEST YOU
LOVE WHO YOU ARE
THINK POSITIVELY

Act like you care:

WRITE YOURSELF A NOTE ABOUT YOU IN ELEMENTARY, MIDDLE, AND
HIGH SCHOOL

RESPECT

RESPECTING SELF
RESPECTING THOSE AROUND YOU.
RESPECTING PROPERTY
YOU HAVE TO CHANGE THE WAY YOU PLAY
NAME PEOPLE WHO RESPECT YOU

Lesson: (A)

ACCEPT CHALLENGES

One Moment Can Change Everything.

You get One Chance Each Day: Make It Count.

Don't always take it personal.

Lesson: (C)
CHOOSING AND WISE CHOICES

When you do not feel good about yourself, and do not believe in yourself, you make choices and choose friends that are in accordance with that low self-esteem.

Self-concept: What we have learned from birth about ourselves?

Self-Image: Include all the positive and negative stuff we learned and taken to heart.

Body Imagery: the concept how we feel about or body.

We learn and are shaped by people who care for us and the people in our environment. We learn to believe in ourselves when we sense others believe in us as beings.

HOW CAN I HANDLE

Frustrations

Fighting

Flipping Out

Pride

I am not a thug. Or do I have thuggish behavior?

Academic struggles

Personal Goals

LABEL YOUR BRAIN AND DESCRIBE WHAT IS IN IT.

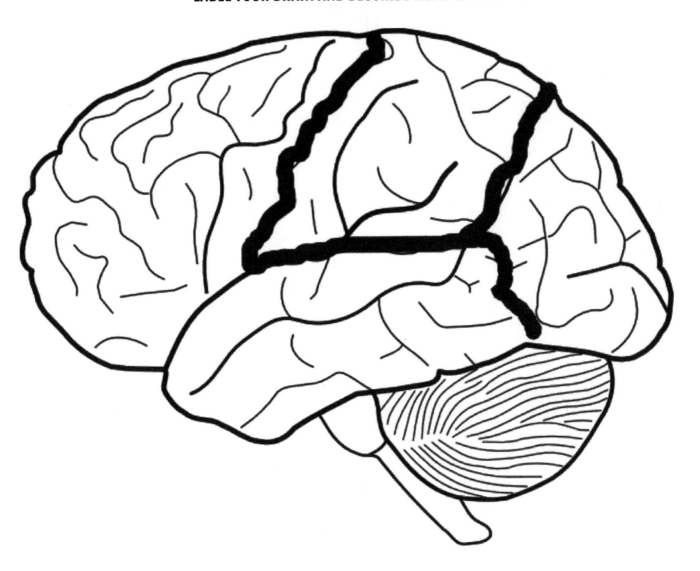

Lesson: (1)

TRUST

TRUST LEVELS

1#Low Levels of Trust happens when relationship promises are broken.
2#Low Levels of Trust causes lying and small actions of betrayal
3#Truth and keeping promise rebuild the broken relationship.
4#High levels of trust happens when you are consistent with step 3#
5# People can count on me

Lesson: (E)

EXCELLENCE AND EXPECTATIONS

You have been given the task of being the principal of your school. You have to solve the problem of the bullying, fighting, detentions, and disrespect of students toward the staff. How would you solve the problem?

What are the Schools Goals?

How would you as principal "Raise the Bar" in the educational environment?

Name Your Preparation Strategies?

What happen when the student is Making a scene during correction?

In the space below, describe the problem as you see it?

Discuss the results.

RISE ABOVE

List (5) Personal obstacles

Define Systemic obstacles: Racism, Poverty, Classism, Mis-placed Anger

1 Anger
I can tell you are hurt about:

I sense you're feeling angry about this situation.

2 Anger is a normal emotion.
Explosive anger is when the natural anger is out of control or unmanageable anger.

3 Steps toward resolving anger.
When you feel angry. You can STOP.

How can I stop?

I can ask myself: Are my emotions in control?

Hypothetical Situations

1. You are blamed for something you did not do.
2. Mom or dad lost their job.
3. You are harassed in the hallway at school about _____.
4. Students laugh at you when you offer the wrong answer to a question.
5. It's your first day back to school after a month-long drug and alcohol program.

6. Your best friend texted the boy/girl you have a crush on?
7. You don't get much sleep at home because your house is too loud.
8. Someone posted a mean tag about you on social media.

How can my actions are a form of Mental Entrapment or Emotional Slavery.

Correction.
Make it right.
Redo.
Do something right.
Check.
Fake it till you make.
Impulsive.
Routine.

NOW CREATE YOUR OWN PERSONAL T-SHIRT IN THE SPACE BELOW

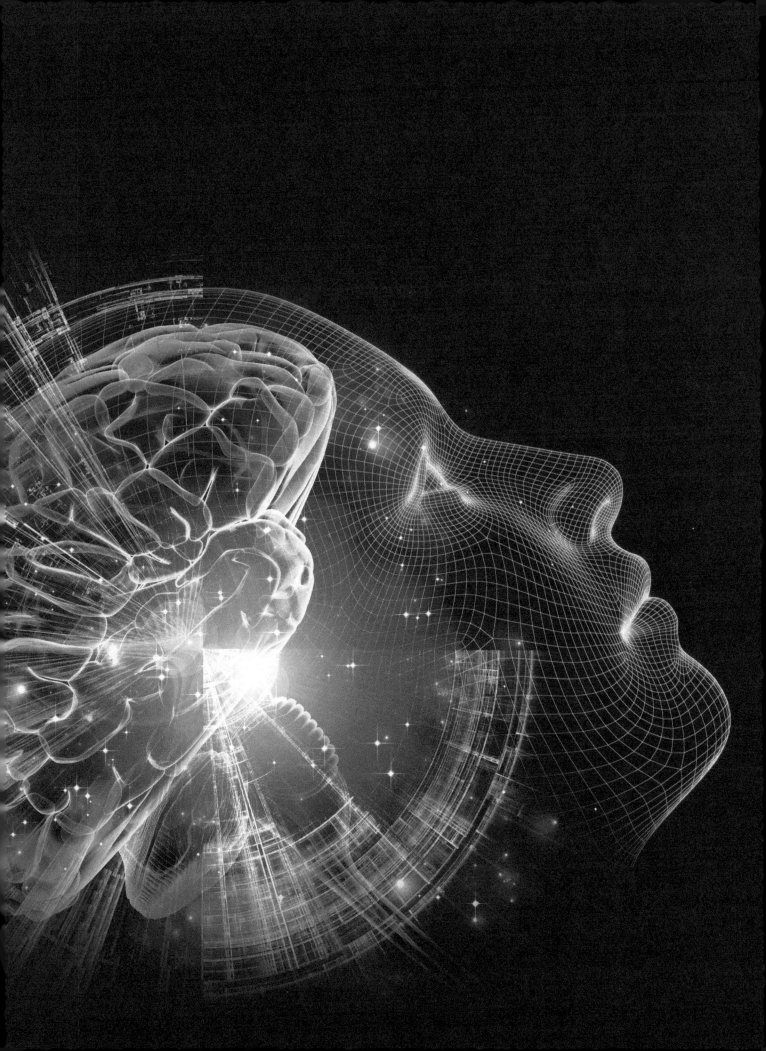

Additional Activities

L1

HOT BUTTON LESSON

Create a Slide presentation in Microsoft PowerPoint using words to describe your emotional hot buttons. As you describe the emotions, be specific about what might trigger these emotions. Triggers can be people, places, and things.

Create one positive solution to improve your response?

Abandoned	Confused	Envious	Ignored	Mad	Sad
Amused	Concerned	Exasperated	Imposed	Miserable	Scared
Annoyed	Crushed	Exhausted	Impressed	Nervous	Silly
Anxious	Defeated	Excited	Indifferent	Outraged	Spiteful
Ashamed	Delighted	Fearful	Infuriated	Overwhelmed	Tense
Bitter	Despairing	Foolish	Inspired	Panicked	Unsettled
Blue	Disconnected	Frightened	Isolated	Pleased	Upset
Bored	Distraught	Guilt	Joy	Pressed	Vulnerable
Burdened	Disturb	Glad	Jealous	Proud	Weary
Calm	Disgusted	Happy	Lonely	Rejected	
Cheated	Eager	Helpful	Low	Restless	
Cheerful	Empty	Hurt			

L2

ANGER

Anger is a normal emotion.

Explosive anger is out of control or unmanageable anger.

When you feel angry, work to **Stop.**

Anger is a form of emotional expression.

Anger can be a form of **destructive intent.**

Anger can be displayed in name calling, using social stereotypes, and forms of racism.

Anger can be displayed on social media sites.

L3

PEER PRESSURE

Peer pressure is a form of peer responses designed to get one to act in a certain way.

Teens in middle school go through the need to belong: Leader or Follower?

1. Communicate well by using your words and expressing your personal boundaries.

2. Resolve conflict quickly. Use a trusted adult to help.

3. Make New friends

4. Learn from other cultures within the school.

5. Be Confident

6. Trust yourself and learn to make good decisions.

7. Work through the emotion of fear of being rejected or criticized with an adult

8. If you feel unsafe, please share with a trusted adult.

L4

DECISIONS

Hazy vision
1. State the situation
2. Options
3. Weigh all the outcomes
4. Is your decision an ethical one?
5. Is this a helpful decision?
6. What are the considered values?
7. Is it lawful?

Things that affect your decisions:

Peer pressure: influence from those your age: Negative

Mindset: your mind, thinking patterns, how you process information

L5

TYPES OF AGGRESSION

Aggression is hostile attention or behavior with intent to harm emotionally, physically, and/or psychologically.

Indirect Aggression: Rumors or Gossip

Direct Aggression: Intending to Harm

Emotional Aggression: My feelings are hurt and I am acting these emotions out.

Hostile Aggression: To inflict harm: verbal/physical (I want you to feel this)

Instrumental Aggression: War for cause or a goal. Hurting another to accomplish a goal.

Things that influence our aggression:
    Exposure to violence
    Group influence
    Frustration
    Comparing self with others

NAME A RECENT EVENT WHERE AGGRESSION WAS PORTRAYED.

L6

SELF DESTRUCTION

Thoughts, feelings, actions.

Inside thoughts produce feelings that create outside behaviors.

All positive thoughts produce positive outcomes.

Who is my circle of influence?

Dealing with negativity and self-defeating thought.

Dealing with people who may be jealous.

PTSD creates stress in our lives.

What is friendship?

How are you when things are not going the way you plan?

What do you do to keep your dream alive?

How do you keep going when all odds are against you?

What is fear?

Determination?

L7

WEAK CHARACTER

Embarrassment. Unable to face denial or rejection

Frustration with aggression. Unable to handle conflict in a healthy way.

Actions: anger, annoyed. Make excuses to move forward, worrying what others think.

Strong need to please others

Respond to situation indecisive. Unable to make up mind

Constant Negativity holding on to things.

Remember: We navigate our lives.

L8

SCHISMS

Describe racism:

Give an example of you experiencing discrimination:

Name some fears associated with racism, discrimination, and labeling persons:

How do you describe disrespect?

How can classes of people disrespect one another?

Why is fairness important today?

Describe what fairness looks like to you:

Respect: I chose to...

Why is respect important in building relationships?

Is Racism a **choice** or is it **learned behavior**? Or can it be **both**?

What are you willing to do in school to combat racism and differences?

L9

FRUSTRATION

Discouragement is a state of being defeated with barriers and hindrances

PLEASE GIVE 3# EXAMPLES
Emotional Pain (inside-outside)

Attack or the perception of being attack

Mad people

L10

IT MATTERS

"Five S"
SELF CARE:
SELF-DEFEATING
SELF-FULFILLING
SABOTAGE
SUCCESS

Are you Coping = dealing with it or Co-existing= I am just here
Are you Conforming= do it because someone else.
How are you expressing your (inside or outside) Emotions= fight- drink-get high-heavy & risky behaviors

DON'T BE MEAN or DON'T BE MAD: Misery, Spiteful, Unkind, Wicked, Selfish.

L11

WHO CARES

Fighting: Who was the first person you saw fighting? What is fight?

Pain: How does your family express pain? How do your community express pain.

Hope: Is hope real?

Mad: How do you handle Mad Behavior?

Sorry: Is sorry a bad word? Why is it not used in school?

Slavery: Name the types of slavery?

PERCEPTION: Is not reality, based on actions, doing, we live in a culture of attention: Cool to be BAD

Bad Attitude Daily
Fighting Reality Shows
Social Media
Drama
Plastic Surgery
Emotions

L12

TRIGGERS AND CHOICES

Learning to Express Healthy Emotions

1. Recognize that I have feelings.
    This morning I felt...
    Sadness + definition of sadness.
    Name your three emotions and define them.

2. Beware of nonverbal emotions
    What are <u>nonverbal emotions</u>?

3. Don't ignore what you are <u>feeling.</u> Never exaggerate feelings. Accept and think about them.

4. Expand emotional vocabulary
    Pick four of the words below and explain:

Elated	Fraudulent
Resilient	Derogatory
Validate	Subordinate
Enthusiastic	Eradicate
Demeanor	Devastated

5. Emotions are messy. Express them without being judgmental

6. Think before you act and/or rush to respond......

L13

RULES FOR HEALTHY FRIENDSHIPS

1. Support each other in positive ways, trust one another: knowing that trust has to be built and earned: it takes two, and be honest but not messy.

2. Listen to your **friends** but challenge your friend to choose wisely even when the decision is not popular

3. No judgments, Friends should not compete. Friends should encourage one another.

4. Don't talk behind a friend's back, whether it's through social media, cell-phones, or conversations.

5. Respect your **friends** — and their boundaries. Friends can have other friends.

6. Ride-or-Die friendships are not healthy. Friendship are built on positivity.

7. Be careful not to Ghost someone who is said to be your friend.

8. Work through conflict and negativity.

Appendix

INTERVENTIONS

Fact: Cognitive ability changes and dynamic of cortical thickness development in healthy children and adolescents, according to Miquel Burgaleta. Healthy adults help students with cognitive flexibility, developing strategies for behaviors and consequences. Without instructions, the adolescent is more prone to high-risk behaviors. Students are incapable of self-regulating the moods without corrective instructions. Adults should model and not react.

The 3-2-1 Behavioral Tracking and Character Monitoring Intervention

Teachers:

The 3-2-1 Behavioral Tracking and Character Monitoring Intervention is a simple tracking system using the numbers 3-2-1 to identify targeted behaviors of a student in a classroom setting. **This Intervention is often used for seventh grade students in middle school.** A small sample of students here at (**school name)** will be monitored on certain targeted behaviors. The tracking data will be collected and used to create long-term positive interventions for the student's success. Each tracking sheet is individualized, uniquely tailored for the student.

The student should be given the option to identify four of his or her behaviors that are tracked during a class period. The student will be responsible for their tracking sheets. If the student is incapable of self-monitoring, the teacher or a team teacher may do so. At the end of the class period, the teacher will be asked to mark **3-2-1.** At the end of the day, each student has a teacher who will be responsible for collecting the folder. On Monday of the following week, the students are to take the weekly tracking sheet home, getting it signed by their parent.

This tracking progress will be used to target specific classroom behaviors, creating a positive solution-focused intervention. This tracking and monitoring progress is used as a clear indicator for student and parent to create positive classroom expectations. It will also identify behaviors that are more apparent in the class period, helping teachers strategize to improve the target behavior with the students. This also prevents categorizing and/or labeling all behaviors as one. Please note: this method is not a reward-based method, it is adopted from a brief solutions-focused model, combined with a strengths perspective.

3. Appropriate Behavior
2. Indicates student used three or more
1. Indicates three or more cues or redirections

GRANTED PERMISSION TO COPY
SAMPLE 3-2-1 Tracker

Daily Tracking Sheet: Date: _____, M T W Th F (circle

Behavior 3= appropriate behavior 2= 2 or less cues 1= 3 or more cues	Husky Time	2nd Encore	3rd Encore	4th Science	5th Math	6th ELA	7th Social Studies
Schedule Breaks							
I can act appropriately with adults. (NO: arguing, refusal, talking under my Breath, cursing)	3 2 1	3 2 1	3 2 1	3 2 1	3 2 1	3 2 1	3 2 1
I can stay focused and stay off my phone. 3 - NO phone reminders 2 - One reminder to put phone away 0 -Two or more reminders	3 2 0	3 2 0	3 2 0	3 2 0	3 2 0	3 2 0	3 2 0
I can (and DID!) complete classwork.	3 2 1	3 2 1	3 2 1	3 2 1	3 2 1	3 2 1	3 2 1
MY TOTAL PER CLASS:	/9	/9	/9	/9	/9	/9	/9
Teacher Requested Breaks:	In: Out:	In: Out:	In: Out:	In: Out:	In: Out:	In: Out:	In: Out:
Teacher Initials							

My Goal is to get 50 points per day. If I get less than 50 points, I will spend the first three class periods with Dr. Dorsey the following day.

137

Fact: Tracking Behavioral Intervention has proven successful. Please be mindful: The more adverse experiences-traumatized children have an underdeveloped frontal lobe and overdeveloped fight or flight reflex. This combination can make it extremely difficult to stay composed during stressful class time and on task in class.

All behavior is not the same but behavior is a clear indicator something is going on. Remember the goal is to decrease behavioral interventions by the eighth grade. The student should have made significant progress to not need a behavioral intervention. Choices and limits go hand in hand. Be careful what you offer, don't take way privilege once offered. Do not include loss of privilege as a threat.

Check-In Check-Out should be used for students who have **Attention Seeking Behavior**
- Cheerful comments — or compliments
- Brief conversations with students
- Helping out with task

Consequence Mapping is for students who are overtly defiant and displaying disrespectful behavior.

Student-Teacher **Contracts** can be used for several behaviors, task avoidance/off task/class disruptions. All STCs should always outline the specific targeted behaviors and classroom goals, involving student as well as parent.

Behavioral Strike system or Tally system outlines the target behaviors used for managing classroom disruptions.

Behavioral Visual Aid with Colors or Objects, Sport Theme, etc. Teachers, you can be as creative as possible. Can be used for students with IEP, ADHD, or other diagnoses.

Strikes with Built-in Breaks for students with severe trauma or other diagnoses.

GRANTED PERMISSION TO COPY

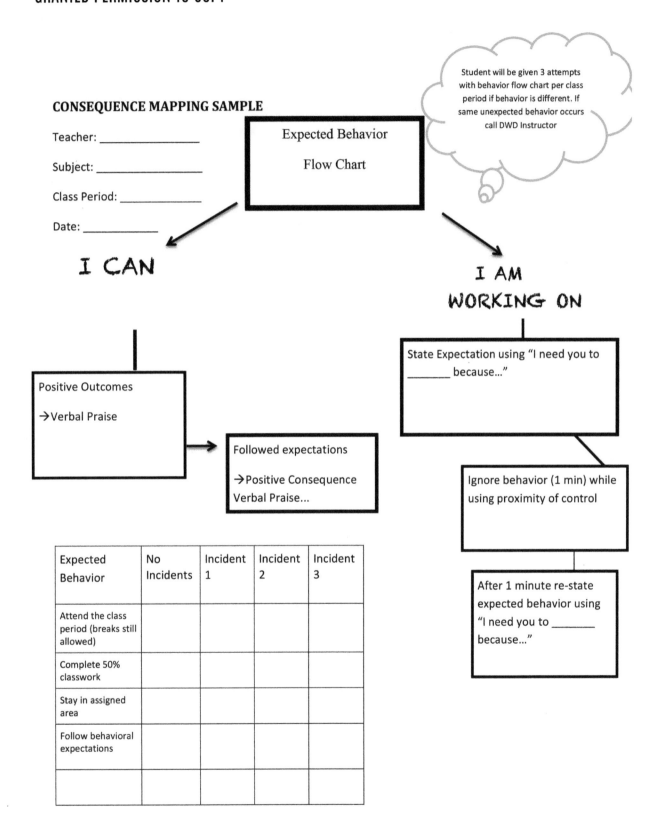

CONSEQUENCE MAPPING SAMPLE

Teacher: _____

Subject: _____

Class Period: _____

Date: _____

Student will be given 3 attempts with behavior flow chart per class period if behavior is different. If same unexpected behavior occurs call DWD Instructor

Expected Behavior

Flow Chart

I CAN

I AM WORKING ON

Positive Outcomes

→Verbal Praise

Followed expectations

→Positive Consequence Verbal Praise...

State Expectation using "I need you to _____ because..."

Ignore behavior (1 min) while using proximity of control

After 1 minute re-state expected behavior using "I need you to _____ because..."

Expected Behavior	No Incidents	Incident 1	Incident 2	Incident 3
Attend the class period (breaks still allowed)				
Complete 50% classwork				
Stay in assigned area				
Follow behavioral expectations				

Consequences for not following expected behavior:	

Reaches the end of the flow chart sent down to Room 100N
   1)   Reflection Sheet
   2)   Reflection Sheet and Call home
   3) Reflection Sheet and Office with referral	

Unexpected Behavior→Use flow chart	**Unexpected Behavior→Automatic Call**
• Yelling out (topic—off subject) • Inappropriate language • Throwing objects • Wandering around room	• Throwing objects at someone • Threatening student or teacher • Standing on table or chair • "using verbal curse words and yelling you're not my dad"

*Student will be given the option to spend an additional period in the social-emotional classroom to complete classwork, he must choose between one block of ELA, Science or Math class at the beginning of the day.

Notes:

_____

_____

_____

_____

_____

ADDITIONAL RESOURCES

Having ADHD along with a coexisting disruptive behavior disorder (ODD/CD) can complicate diagnosis and treatment and also worsen the prognosis. Even though many children with ADHD ultimately adjust. Oftentimes schools use the diagnosis of OHI.

What are other types of (OHI) disruptive behavior disorders?

According to DSM (Diagnostic and Statistical Manual of Mental Disorders), disruptive behavior disorders include two similar disorders: oppositional defiant disorder (ODD) and conduct disorder (CD). Common symptoms occurring in children with these disorders include: defiance of authority figures, angry outbursts, and other antisocial behaviors such as lying and stealing

Oppositional defiant disorder (ODD) refers to a recurrent pattern of negative, defiant, disobedient and hostile behavior toward authority figures lasting at least six months. To be diagnosed with ODD four (or more) of the following symptoms must be present:
- often loses temper
- often argues with adults
- often actively defies or refuses to comply with adults' requests or rules
- often deliberately annoys people
- often blames others for his or her mistakes or misbehavior
- is often touchy or easily annoyed by others
- is often angry and resentful
- is often spiteful or vindictive.

Conduct disorder (CD) involves more serious behaviors including aggression toward people or animals, destruction of property, lying, stealing and skipping school. The behaviors associated with CD are often described as delinquency.

GRANTED PERMISSION TO COPY

Good character consists of understanding, caring about, and acting upon core ethical values. Character education is a way of being, and most notably, a way of being with others. –Dr. Marvin W. Berkowitz

MIDDLE SCHOOL REFLECTION SHEET NAME_____

Background: XXX

The Actors: XXX

STOP! Are my emotions in control? Do I have a dilemma? (Describe the Problem)

_____

_____

Think!

What are my choices?	What character trait would be demonstrated?	How does the ....apply?
1.		
2.		
3.		
4.		

ACT! What character trait do I choose to demonstrate? What choices will I make?

_____

_____

What supporting character or skill will I need to act on my choice? Do I need to ask for help?

_____

_____

Classroom Environment:

STUDENT PROFILE 2000

Teachers please use the below information as a positive support for students in the academic setting. The information below is not used for punitive purposes. All information collected by the EIP Social-Emotional Staff to provide education supports.

Student Name

IEP Supports

Grade Level

Level Counselor

Trauma Strategies
- ✓ Self-Regulating Strategies

Identified Student Triggers
- ✓

Practical Strategies Used
- ✓ Classroom Re-entry after cool down
- ✓ Academic Advocacy
- ✓ Trauma and the Brain
- ✓ Adverse Child Experience
- ✓ Regulation
- ✓ De-escalation Strategies
- ✓ Established a routine of breaks

Student's Narrative

Submitted by

GRANTED PERMISSION TO COPY

EXAMPLE OF SCHOOL STUDENT CRISIS PLAN

Recommendation: (The Student) will be placed in the _____for the morning session. _____will work within the **Trauma** classroom during the afternoon. _____ will be allowed to attend one class (computers) in the afternoon. However, supervision to and from the alternative program must be in place for the student to attend the computer class.

- Morning check-in with Counselor immediately following arrival to school. (Back-up supports:
- Daily checking of backpack to make sure no weapons are present.
- Student will be given daily assignments from classroom teachers to keep up with required coursework. (Modifications will be made for assignments requiring class participation.)
- Student should be given instruction in social skills: seeking adult assistance, handling frustration and making positive choices
- Student should be given a crisis pass if he is feeling stressed out.
- Student should sit in front of room and near teacher or bus driver in classroom/bus.
- Student should not attend a class where there is a substitute teacher. Alternate plans should be made on these days.
- Breakfast and lunch should be provided in the alternative center with no cafeteria privileges at this point.
- Speech pathologist will come to the alternative center on a weekly basis to provide required services.

Team Review: A meeting will be scheduled with parents to review the student's progress during the first week in May. Counselor should keep in contact with the outside therapist regarding changes in behavior or progress made.

ACES QUESTION/TOOL

Prior to your 18th birthday:

1. Did a parent or other adult in the household often or very often: Swear at you, insult you, put you down, or humiliate you? Act in a way that made you afraid that you might be physically hurt?

   No___ If Yes, enter 1 __

2. Did a parent or other adult in the household often or very often: Push, grab, slap, or throw something at you? Ever hit you so hard that you had marks or were injured?

   No___ If Yes, enter 1 __

3. Did an adult or person at least five years older than you ever: Touch or fondle you or have you touch their body in a sexual way? Attempt or actually have oral, anal, or vaginal intercourse with you?

   No___ If Yes, enter 1 __

4. Did you often or very often feel that: No one in your family loved you or thought you were important or special? Your family didn't look out for each other, feel close to each other, or support each other?

   No___ If Yes, enter 1 __

5. Did you often or very often feel that: You didn't have enough to eat, had to wear dirty clothes, and had no one to protect you? Your parents were too drunk or high to take care of you or take you to the doctor if you needed it?

   No___ If Yes, enter 1 __

6. Were your parents ever separated or divorced?

   No___ If Yes, enter 1 __

7. Was your mother or stepmother: Often or very often pushed, grabbed, slapped, or had something thrown at her? Sometimes, often, or very often kicked, bitten, hit with a fist, or hit with something hard? Ever repeatedly hit over at least a few minutes or threatened with a gun or knife?

   No___ If Yes, enter 1 __

8. Did you live with anyone who was a problem drinker or alcoholic, or who used street drugs?

   No___ If Yes, enter 1 __

9. Was a household member depressed or mentally ill, or did a household member attempt suicide?

   No___ If Yes, enter 1 __

10. Did a household member go to prison?

    No___ If Yes, enter 1 __

Now add up your "Yes" answers: _ This is your ACE Score

RESILIENCE QUESTIONNAIRE

Please circle the most accurate answer <u>under</u> each statement:

1. I believe that my mother loved me when I was little.

Definitely true—Probably true—Not sure—Probably Not True—Definitely Not True

2. I believe that my father loved me when I was little.

Definitely true—Probably true—Not sure—Probably Not True—Definitely Not True

3. When I was little, other people helped my mother and father take care of me and they seemed to love me.

Definitely true—Probably true—Not sure—Probably Not True—Definitely Not True

4. I've heard that when I was an infant someone in my family enjoyed playing with me, and I enjoyed it, too.

Definitely true—Probably true—Not sure—Probably Not True—Definitely Not True

5. When I was a child, there were relatives in my family who made me feel better if I was sad or worried.

Definitely true—Probably true—Not sure—Probably Not True—Definitely Not True

6. When I was a child, neighbors or my friends' parents seemed to like me.

Definitely true—Probably true—Not sure—Probably Not True—Definitely Not True

7. When I was a child, teachers, coaches, youth leaders or ministers were there to help me.

Definitely true—Probably true—Not sure—Probably Not True—Definitely Not True

8. Someone in my family cared about how I was doing in school.

Definitely true—Probably true—Not sure—Probably Not True—Definitely Not True

9. My family, neighbors and friends talked often about making our lives better.

Definitely true—Probably true—Not sure—Probably Not True—Definitely Not True

10. We had rules in our house and were expected to keep them.
Definitely true—Probably true—Not sure—Probably Not True—Definitely Not True

11. When I felt really bad, I could almost always find someone I trusted to talk to.
Definitely true—Probably true—Not sure—Probably Not True—Definitely Not True

12. As a youth, people noticed that I was capable and could get things done.
Definitely true—Probably true—Not sure—Probably Not True—Definitely Not True

13. I was independent and a go-getter.
Definitely true—Probably true—Not sure—Probably Not True—Definitely Not True

14. I believed that life is what you make it.
Definitely true—Probably true—Not sure—Probably Not True—Definitely Not True

How many of these fourteen protective factors did I have as a child and youth? (How many of the fourteen were circled "Definitely True" or "Probably True"?) _____

ENDNOTES

1 Wells, Adrian. (2000). *Emotional Disorders & Metacognition: Innovative Cognitive Therapy*. University of Manchester, UK: John Wiley .& Sons.

2 Jensen, Frances E. (MD)., (08/2016). Presentation at MICDS. *The Teenage and Young Adult Brain: Neuroscience You Can Use*. The University of Pennsylvania. Perelman School of Medicine

3 Jensen, Frances E., Nutt, Amy E. (2014). *The Teenage Brain, A Neuroscientist's Survival Guide to Raising Adolescents and Young Adults*. Harper Collins Publications.

4 Treatment for Posttraumatic Stress Disorder in Military and Veteran Populations: Final Assessment. Institute of Medicine. June 2014.

5 Hodges, L. F., Rothbaum, B. O., Kooper, R., Opdyke, D., Meyer T., North, M., de Graff, J. J., & Williford, J. (1995). *Virtual environments for exposure therapy*. IEEE Computer Journal, July, 27-34

6 Curwin, Richard., Mendler, Allen N., Mendler, Brian, D., (2008), *Discipline with Dignity*. Association for Supervision and Curriculum Development. Alexandria, Virginia.

7 Jensen, Frances E., Nutt, Amy E. (2014). *The Teenage Brain, A Neuroscientist's Survival Guide to Raising Adolescents and Young Adults*. Harper Collins Publications.

8 Normal Development of Cognition and the Brain–Children .... *https://www. lawandmotherhood.com/children-memory/normal-development-of-cognition-and-the-brain.html*

9 Paus T., Zijdenbos A., Worsley K., Collins DL., Blumenthal J., Giedd JN., Rapoport JL., Evans AC Science. 1999 Mar 19; 283(5409): 1908-11.

10 https://www.cmu.edu/homepage/health/2013/fall/absorbing-information.shtml

11 Bratsberg, Bert., Rogeberg, (2018). *Flynn effect and its reversal are both environmentally caused*. PNAS (Proceedings of the National Academy of Science of the United States of America) June 26., 115 (26) 6674-6678; first published June 11, 2018 https://doi.org/10.1073/pnas.1718793115

12 Expanding Minds Opportunity https://www.expandinglearning.org/sites/default/files/em_articles/1_buildingaculture.pdf

13 Jensen, Frances E., Nutt, Amy E. (2014). *The Teenage Brain, A Neuroscientist's Survival Guide to Raising Adolescents and Young Adults*. Harper Collins Publications

14 Ibid.

15 Morey RA, Gold AL, LaBar KS, et al. (2012). Amygdala volume changes in post-traumatic stress disorder in a large case-controlled veterans group. *Arch Gen Psychiatry*. 69(11):1169–1178. doi:10.1001/archgenpsychiatry.2012.50

16 Wells, Adrian. (2000). *Emotional Disorders & Metacognition: Innovative Cognitive Therapy*. University of Manchester, UK: John Wiley & Sons.

17 Durand F., Isaac C., Januel D. (2019). Emotional memory in post-traumatic stress disorder: a systematic PRISMA review of controlled studies. *Front Psychol.*;10:303. doi:10.3389/fpsyg.00303

18 Van de Kolk, Bessell. (2014). *The Body Keeps the Score: Brain, Mind, and Body in the Healing of Trauma*. Penguin,: Random House LLC. New York.

19 Beyond Adversity: Addressing the mental health needs of young people who face complexity and adversity in their lives. Addressing mental health and well-being in young people. CentreForum(2016)Commission on Children & Young People's Mental health State of the Nation: http://centreforum.org/live/wp-content/uploads/2016/04/ State-of the-Nation-report-web.pdf.

20 Ibid.

21 Kennedy, Randall. (2002). *Nigger-The Strange Career of a Troublesome Word*. Cahners Business Information..

22 Dickerson, Joshua T., (2016). Cause I ain't got a pencil. Jax Publication.

23 Curwin, Richard., Mendler, Allen N., Mendler, Brian, D., (2008), *Discipline with Dignity*. Association for Supervision and Curriculum Development. Alexandria, Virginia

24 Jacobs, Majorie., Turk, Blossom, Horn, Elizabeth Horn. (1988). *Building a Positive Self-Concept*. J. Weston, Walch; Portland, Maine.ix

25 Waldman, Mark Robert.,Newberg, Andrew B., (2012*). Words Can Change Your Brain:12 Conversation Strategies to Build Trust Resolve Conflict and Increase Intimacy*. Penguin Publishing Group. New York.

26 Jacobs, Majorie., Turk, Blossom, Horn, Elizabeth Horn. (1988).

27 Ibid.

28 Rapper Smoke D of UGK, March 2017 Interview. *Happy Death Day: Lives & Death of UGK's Smoke D:* **Memoir**

29 Jacobs, Majorie., Turk, Blossom, Horn, Elizabeth Horn. (1988).

30 Forbes, Heather T. (2017). *Help for Billy*. Trauma-Informed Classroom's Notes: By Heather T. Forbes *www.TheTraumaInformedSchool.com.,* www.BeyondConsequences.com, Beyond Consequences

31 Young, Kathleen. (2018). *Treating Trauma in Tucson: How Trauma Impacts Mental Health*. May 18,. https://drkathleenyoung.wordpress.com/2010/05/18/how-trauma-impacts-mental-health/

32 Ibid.

33 Center of Developing Child: Harvard University. https://developingchild.harvard.edu/

34 Ibid.

35 Lauer, John. (2017). *Epigenetic for dummies*. April 28,.group.dmj.com., https://www.researchgate.net/publication/297736437_Epigenetics_for_dummies

36 https://www.narcotics.com/opioids/opioids-affect-brain/

37 *https://childmind.org/article/how-to-give-kids-effective-instructions/*

38 Reichart, Micheal., Hawley, Richard. (2010). *Reaching Boys & Teaching Boys, Strategies that Work-Why.* A. Wiley Imprint. Jossey-Bass, San Francisco, CA.

39 Kunjufu, Jawanza. (2005). Countering the Conspiracy to Destroy Black Boys Series. Fourteenth Printing

40 Ruef, Michael B., Higgins, Cindy., Glaeser, Barbara J. C., Patnode, Marianne. (1998). *Positive Behavioral Support:Strategies for teachers.*

41 http://kirwaninstitute.osu.edu/research/understanding-implicit-bias/ The University of Ohio State, 2012 Research. The Implicit Bias Review. December 13.2019.

42 ibid.

43 https://childmind.org/article/how-to-give-kids-effective-instructions/

44 Woolsey-Terrazas, Wendy and Chavez, Janice A. (2012). *Strategies to Work with Students with Oppositional   Defiant Disorder.* Cowin-Thousand Oaks, California.

45 https://childmind.org/article/how-to-give-kids-effective-instructions/

46 Ziv & Dolev, 2013; Goldbeck & Ellerkamp, 2012; Saarikallio & Erkkila, 2007 How music benefits your class or community.https://safesupportivelearning.ed.gov/node/5870/results

47 McDermott & Houser, 2005.

48 Rentfrow & Gosling, 2003.

49 "Study Finds Brain Hub That Links Music, Memory, and Emotion (2009). UC Davis News & Information." UC Davis News & Information. UC Davis, 23 Feb., Web. 03 Apr. 20

50 Gregory AH., (1997). *The roles of music in society*: The ethnomusicological perspective. In: Hargreaves David J, North Adrian C., editors. The social psychology of music. New York, NY, US: Oxford University Press;   1997. pp. 123–140.

51 Koelsch S. (2009). *A neuroscientific perspective on music therapy.* Annals of the New York Academy of Sciences. 1169(1):374–384.

52 Ziv & Dolev, 2013; Goldbeck & Ellerkamp, 2012; Saarikallio & Erkkila, 2007

53 Koelsch S. (2009) *A neuroscientific perspective on music therapy.*

54 Baker, Mitzi. (2007). *Music Moves Brain to Pay Attention.* Stanford School of Medicine. Stanford School of Medicine, 01 Aug. Web. 03 Apr. 2014.

55 Ibid.

56 Christ, Scott. (2014). *20 Surprising, Science-backed Health Benefits of Music."* USA Today. Gannett, 17 Dec. 2013. Web. 03 Apr.

57 Costello, Bob., Wachtel, Joshua, and Ted., (2009). *The Restorative Practice Handbook.* For Teachers, Disciplinarians, and Administrators: Building a Culture of Community in Schools. International Institute for Restorative Practices. Canada.

CPSIA information can be obtained
at www.ICGtesting.com
Printed in the USA
BVHW021403290720
584937BV00019B/551